God put a Dream in my Heart

Handbook of Life Therapy

By

Eva Dillner

1stBooks - rev. 06/13/03

*"**Just about the most useful tool any therapist could have in their toolkit**"*

Carol Logan, President of the International Association for Kairos Therapy

Table of Contents

Introduction

I wrote this book as part of my own process to get clear on my own philosophy of life. To summarize what I really can own from all the teachers I've had, to share what I found useful and most importantly, what has worked for me. In other words a synthesis of my understanding of what it's all about.

I've included many concepts and exercises, my hope is that when my book is published it will become a handbook for personal development. It is in no way intended as a substitute for professional therapy or medical treatment. My recommendation is that you read through the entire book once, before you start working with the material.

Perhaps you are just starting your journey - do the exercises that feel right for you. Some you can do on your own, others you need a partner or a group to get maximum benefit from. If you feel uncomfortable doing the exercises on your own, seek out a therapist or group facilitator you feel comfortable with. It may take some searching, but that is part of the process to learn to trust your inner self.

Perhaps you are a therapist looking for some fresh approaches. Feel free to use what appeals to you and leave the rest. Perhaps your clients want to read the book as an adjunct to therapy. Or you may want to run a weekly group using the exercises to help your clients get more out of their therapy, or as preparation for therapy.

Perhaps you are a workshop leader who will find the book useful as a course textbook.

Meditation is a cornerstone in most of my work. You will notice there isn't a separate chapter on meditation, but that meditative exercises are interspersed throughout the text.

Emotions are energy in motion. To stay healthy we need to move, breathe and experience our emotions. Stress causes shallow breathing. Inactivity slows down the chi or life energy. When we repress emotions they stay in our bodies. When we are unable to fully experience emotions we store them in our bodies and experience them as tension, muscle aches, upset stomachs, migraines, nightmares, tiredness, depression etc. Our bodies natural response to trauma is to shut down as we are unable to cope with the myriad of emotions - but they stay in our bodies until the shock can be released.

I believe God put a Dream in every human being's Heart, and that we are here on earth to remember and manifest that dream. The trick is to let go of logical thinking and allow magical thinking in, long enough to inspire us to action. As we step onto our true path, all the baggage that stands in our way to achieve the Dream pops out like a Jack in the Box. That's why it's so important to do therapy because then we eliminate the obstacles that keep us from getting what we want.

So this book is about becoming more ourselves. As we clear out the baggage, we connect with our true dreams and can start to realize them. But no amount of therapy can take the step for you. Therapy removes the obstacles and opens the cage door, but it is your responsibility to take the step and walk out of the cage. Only then will you know what the outcome is. Let go of your attachment to the outcome, it seldom turns out the way you pictured it. I have a plan, but it usually turns out that God had a better plan.

And stepping out of the cage often brings up another layer to be worked through. It's as if we can only progress so far while in a certain situation. Leaving the situation is the only way to free up the next layer. Or if we let ourselves really feel our situation, we would have to leave it.

I've chosen to call this process Life Therapy.

Whereas traditional medicine is excellent for broken bones, acute illnesses and surgeries, Life Therapy may help you when the symptoms are diffuse or where no clear medical or psychiatric cause can be established. Life Therapy can help you release tension, heal emotional wounds from minor incidents as well as deeper trauma, improve your emotional and physical well being and deepen your spiritual connection.

You can take the Life Therapy training
　　　—for your own personal growth
　　　—to become a therapist
　　　—to train as a teacher

A little bit about me. I started out as an engineer and worked in the corporate world for fifteen years with project management and organizational change in the USA and France. By the end of 1990, after umpteen cutbacks and efficiency improvements I was burned out. Too chicken to quit, I took a leave of absence, which ended with me getting laid off. So, too exhausted to cope with much of anything, I slowly started my quest to get my life back. I've trained with many of the pioneers in the personal growth and therapy movement in the United States and Europe. My training has included Kairos®/Shen Therapy,

Hypnotherapy, Life Energy Fundamentals, Meditation, Personal Growth, Secret of Creating Your Future®, Hawaiian Huna, Gemstone Therapy, Life Mission, Sound Meditation, Personal Presence®, Yoga, Hawaiian Lomi-Lomi Massage, Release Dancing and Vedic Art®. Since 1998 I live in Sweden, where I was born and raised. My company is named Divine Design, inspired by the writings of Florence Scovel Shinn. I have been featured in articles in the local as well as national press. More information is available on my website www.divinedesign.nu.

Notes:

1) ® denotes a registered trademark of a name granted for a specific time period by a country.

2) The Shen organization split into two in 2002, the new branch is called Kairos Therapy.

Awareness

The two main factors in determining the outcome of therapy is the client's ability and willingness to stay present with whatever their bodies bring up and surrendering to the process, and the therapist's ability and willingness to take the client where they need to go. I think we need to train clients in presence, awareness and surrender. As therapists we need to work through our own material. We can only take our clients as far as we ourselves are willing to go. So let's start with awareness.

Weather Report

One of my favorite exercises for awareness is the weather report. Just like the weather can be sunny or cloudy, calm or stormy; you too can experience many different states of "weather". Let yourself sit comfortably in a chair. Close your eyes. Take a few deep breaths, let yourself relax into the chair, and start to notice, become aware of your present state - not what happened today or what you think might happen tomorrow, but right now, in this very moment, what are you aware of? First focus on your physical body - is there any particular area drawing your attention? Do you notice any pain, tingles or other sensations? Become aware of your breathing - is it full or constricted? If it's tight, just notice where. Continue focusing on the body until it feels complete. Next focus on your mind. What is going on right now. Is there a lot of chatter, is there a theme, or is it congested or just parked? The possibilities are endless, just notice what is going on in your mind right now. Continue being aware of your mind until it feels complete. Next focus your awareness on your current emotional state. Do you feel upset, anxious, sad or calm and harmonious. There is no right way to feel, just notice what is going on with your emotions right now, perhaps you experience being unsure of how to do this exercise.

You can't do it right. You can't do it wrong. You can only be yourself.

Continue being aware of your emotions until it feels complete. Next shift your awareness to your spiritual connection. Do you feel connected to Spirit? or do you feel like God is on vacation and left you hanging? Just notice what you are aware of right now. Continue focusing your awareness on your spiritual connection until it feels complete. Take a few deep breaths, wiggle your fingers and toes, stretch and open your eyes.

Do this exercise as frequently as you like. You'll discover that it's different every time, just like the weather.

A bit more on *You can't do it right. You can't do it wrong. You can only be yourself.* Each person's experience in doing an exercise is different. Some people are by nature more descriptive or experience a multitude of senses, others have an experience that is soft and gentle, perhaps with just a hint of sensation. God made you unique and you are perfect just the way you are. Your experience is your experience and the exercise is not about achieving a particular result like seeing colors, but just to be aware of your inner weather.

Your senses - sight, sound, smell, touch and taste - are doorways to your life purpose as well as your memories.

I stumbled onto the life purpose connection to our senses when I was doing life mission work. A course participant had an idea for a business, but hadn't been able to get going for some reason. In listening to her describe the idea, there was something missing - there was no life energy in it. She sounded very logical and practical, but where was the enthusiasm? When probing her other interests I stumbled onto her enthusiasm for welding. She started describing the perfect weld with an enthusiasm and aliveness that hadn't been there before. She said "when you *look* at a perfect weld it's like a rainbow, shimmering with all the colors". She continued "I love the *smell* of machine shops, when I can't go to sleep at night I imagine the *sound* from arc welding, it's the most soothing *sound* I know".

Amazing, the welder had been there all along, but had gotten buried under other expectations. What sense clues do you have hidden within you? Before we do another exercise to access your sense clues, we need to talk about attention and intention. Intention sets the course, attention helps you pick up the clues you need to navigate. For example, if your stated intention is to understand your life mission, you will start to get answers and indicators that match that intention. If your stated intention is to understand why you are stuck, you will most likely get indicators leading to a memory or memories that need to be therapeutically resolved before you can move on. If the answers you get feel empty or show stillness in nature pictures, then most likely that is what you need to focus on for the time being. When the time is ready, you will know what to do. There is a time for being too. I think we have lost the fine art of staring into space. A very useful skill in personal growth work, just being. For really advanced "being" get a hammock! It's my personal favorite.

Sense Clues

Getting in touch with your senses exercise. Turn off the phone and tell your family to not disturb you. Before you start, get clear on your intention, state your question - I want to understand my life mission, or I want to know why I have trouble standing up for myself, or I want to know what would be good for me right now, are just some of the examples of intentions to use. Get comfortable, sit with spine straight in a chair, or lie down on the floor. Close your eyes. Take a few slow deep breaths. Feel your feet, let them relax. Feel your ankles, let them relax. Move your attention up your legs and body, become aware of the sensations in your body at each stop, and relax. Do this all the way to the top of the head. Continue breathing softly and deeply, letting yourself go deeper into relaxation with each breath.

Imagine yourself going down a spiral staircase, count the steps as you go down, continue spiralling downward until you feel deeply relaxed and ready to move on to exploring your sense clues. State your intention, repeat it to yourself, out loud if you wish. Then imagine yourself in a space where your visual clues reside. Focus on seeing, become aware of what you see, what pictures or images appear, stay in visual space until you feel ready to move on. Imagine yourself moving to another space, where your hearing or auditory clues reside. If you want you can restate your intention as you move into each new space. Listen, what do you hear, what sounds are there, or absence of certain sounds, just be present and curious, and notice what auditory impulses you get. Stay as long as needed, until you feel it's time to move on. Now transport yourself to the next space, where your feeling clues reside. What do you notice in your body, what do you feel, what kinaesthetic clues appear here, what physical sensation are you aware of? Continue paying attention to feeling clues until it feels done. Now move to the space where smell resides. Sniff the air, what smells come your way, what olfactory senses are awakened, what odours or perfumes fill the air? When smell feels complete, move on to the last space, taste. Let yourself taste, what is your saliva and tongue picking up, is it spicy or mild, bitter, sweet etc, just let yourself take in the taste sensations until it feels done. Now start to come back to here and now, take a few deep breaths, wiggle your fingers and toes, stretch and open your eyes. Write down your answers if you wish. Keeping a journal can be very helpful as you play detective with yourself.

Our senses are also doorways to memory. It's an excellent tool for accessing material to work with in therapy. When I was studying hypnotherapy, much of the focus was on what do you see - but my strongest connector was smell, I could smell where I was and that was my doorway into forgotten memories. In therapy, working with what's on the surface will get you to the next layer. If the client reports physical pain when you ask about how they are feeling emotionally, work with the physical pain, it will eventually dissolve into emotion or some other sensation.

Using all the senses in guided imagery will get you deeper and work faster than just focusing on the visual. Let yourself *see* the colors of the tree, *feel* the breeze, *hear* the rustling of the leaves, experience the *smell* of nature and imagine *tasting* the sap of the tree.

Activating the Biofield

The biofield is simply the life energy that permeates your whole body and extends beyond it to become the aura. There are four main ways I work with life energy to activate the biofield. Through breath and movement, sound, dance and laying on of hands.

Breath and Movement

Breathing helps pump the chi, or life energy through the body. Movement also activates the chi, so when combined the effects can be powerful, for example triggering emotional memories. If you were at one of my workshops I would now introduce some of the breath and movement exercises I've found most useful. But don't despair, they are available on video and are easy to learn on your own. Jane Hundley's Movement and Breath Exercises for Personal Presence take the breath into the whole body. Jane is a corporate personal presence trainer as well as a rebirther who studied with Sondra Ray. Women especially like the circular movements of these exercises which could be described as hula yoga. Benefits include improved sleep, faster recovery from jet lag, and of course increased presence in the here and now. Nancy Zi's Art of Breathing primarily opens up abdominal breathing. Nancy is an opera singer as well as chi kung master and has combined chi kung with exercises from classical singing. She calls the method Chi Yi, or the Art of Breathing. Benefits include improved capacity for singing and speaking and being able to breathe all the way down to the root. When you do these exercises, make sure you exhale completely. It's trapped, stale air in the lungs that causes dizziness when you practice slow and deep breathing.

Sound

Toning, or chanting, not only opens up the biofield or life energy, it also makes you present, connects the two halves of the brain, deepens your breathing, opens up your throat and strengthens your voice.

The sound exercises I will introduce you to here are only the tip of the iceberg. Check out www.soundhealers.com for more info.

Chakra tones open up the biofield. They are more effectful when done in a group, but can be done on your own as well. When clients book appointments after a group toning they need little or no work to break up the tension that is the doorway to stuck emotions.

Chakra Names, Colors, Sounds and Physical Landmarks

First we'll cover the chakra names, colors and sounds:

Chakra	Color	Sound
1 - root	red	uh
2 - sacral	orange	ow
3 - solar plexus	yellow	oh
4 - heart	pink/sea green	ah
5 - throat	sapphire blue	eh
6 - brow	indigo	ay
7 - crown	purple	e

The physical locations of the chakras are as follows:

Physical location	Chakra	Rearward line
base of spine	root (R)	
top of pubic bone		root/sacral (RS)
	sacral (S)	
navel/iliac crest		sacral/solar plexus (SSP)
	solar plexus (SP)	
vee of ribcage/xiphoid		solar plexus/heart (SPH)
	heart (H)	
sternum		heart/throat (HT)
supersternal notch	throat (T)	
mouth/jaws		throat/brow (TB)
center of forehead	brow (B)	
top of head	crown (C)	

So the sacral (S) is located halfway between the top of the pubic bone and the navel/iliac crest line, the throat (T) at the supersternal notch, which is the hollow at the base of the throat. The rearward lines will be explained under laying on of hands. In Kairos/Shen Therapy the face is considered to be one big frontward flow, and the brow chakra is not a separate center. I've chosen to include the brow chakra and indicated the mouth/jaw line as a rearward flow, but I'm not 100% decided of the direction of the flow at the mouth/jaw line. One of my Kairos colleagues has started to include the supersternal notch into the HT rearward and doing the forward flow through the larynx, and has found it to be much more effective.

Chakra Sounds

Now we are ready to start toning the chakras. Sit in a chair or cross-legged on the floor. Get centered and comfortable. Take a few deep breaths. Your body knows how to make the sounds, relax and let the sound come naturally when it is ready. I usually focus on the physical location of the chakra, visualize the color in front of me, and imagine the sound. I just softly breathe into the physical location of the chakra until my body wants to make a sound on the outbreath. Let your whole body relax, toning is effortless. Straining or efforting will only stress your vocal chords. I've had course participants sit through several sessions before their bodies were ready to make a sound. Don't worry, your body will tone when it's ready. Repeat each tone 3 - 7 times. Rest between each tone and just notice how your body feels. Work at your own pace. You may notice that your sound is a bit different each time - that is normal.

HU Sing

Another toning exercise I find useful is to sing HU, pronounced like Hugh, which is an ancient Tibetan chant that means God. Use this when you want spiritual guidance or as a prelude to meditation. Lovely to do in a group for about twenty minutes. One course participant exclaimed "our souls have been longing for us to do this!".

Name Song

A fun exercise is to sing names in a group. It works like this. One person receives, the rest of the group sings. If I am the receiver I start by saying "I want you to sing my name Eva". The group tunes into or feels intuitively how to sing Eva, then sings Eva repetitively until it feels complete. I, as the receiver, focus on how it feels to be bathed in sound. Go around the circle taking turns being sung to. You can expand the exercise by requesting intentions such as "I want you to tone the intention of love" and you may also ask for colors by simply stating "I want you to tone the color purple". Pay attention to how it feels to give and how it feels to receive. Is it different? Is one easier than the other? Imagine if meetings at work started this way?

Humming

If the above exercises feel a bit too scary to start with, you can just hum. Think of a purring cat and just hum. Hmmm... and notice how your body feels.

Dance

A natural way to wake the chakras is through dance, letting the body move freely in what is known as release dancing. Perhaps you are familiar with Gabrielle Roth's work called the Five Rhythms, which is one way to work therapeutically with dance and movement. I prefer to work with the elements - earth, water, fire and air - as they correspond to the chakras and naturally tie into the rest of my work.

Dance is part of who I am. When I was quite young I danced in front of the altar at church. When my staunchly religious grandmother caught up with me and demanded to know what I was doing I replied "I'm celebrating the resurrection of Jesus".

Warm Up

Dancing connects us to who we are deep inside. You'll need comfortable clothes that let you move freely and plenty of fresh water to drink. To warm up you can do some breathing and movement exercises and/or gently pat your body from top to bottom. Pat softly with the whole hand. Start with the head and face, then the neck, shoulders and arms, continue down the front of the torso and down the legs. When you get to the feet, you can massage them gently. Go back up the back of the legs and buttocks. Then pair up and do each others backs, bend forward so the back is horizontal, relax and enjoy.

Skeleton Exercise

An optional exercise that is quite fun to do is to touch the skeleton. Pair up with a partner and stand in a relaxed fashion. If you are receiving, close your eyes, breathe softly and let your awareness follow as your skeleton is palpated by your partner's fingertips. If you are giving, start at the top of the head. Gently let your fingers probe the skeleton, all the bones throughout your partners body. Use common sense and avoid touching sensitive areas like the eyes, nipples or genitals. This exercise increases awareness of the body and helps you get familiar with landmarks, which is useful when you do any kind of bodywork.

You can either dance through the whole body and all the elements, then move onto the table, or you can focus on say the root and dance it, tone it and then get on the table to do root work. Vary and combine as you see fit and time allows.

More Warm Up

If you didn't warm up with some breath and movement, now is the time to gently dance through the body. Put on some gently swaying music and let your body listen and feel. Let your head move in tune to the music, then let your neck and shoulders move with the music, then your arms. Stay with each body part for a while, then move on. Let your fingers feel the music, then your torso, your waist, your hips. Move into your thighs, legs, knees and feet. Connect with the cells in your body, let your mind go, your body knows what it wants to do. Let go. One of my dance teachers always starts with the instruction to remove the head and leave it at the door, at the end of the session we put our heads back on before we head out the door.

The Elements

The element earth corresponds to the root and the legs. The music can be drums, didgeridoos, african rhythms etc. Anything that is earthy, lots of base and lets you stomp your feet. Focus your awareness on your feet, legs and root, let them lead you in the dance and movement. If your body doesn't want to move, just be with it. If you want to curl up in a corner, do that. Just follow whatever your body says it wants to do.

The next element is water, which corresponds with the sacral chakra. The music is flowing and fluid, like a Viennese waltz. Let your hips sway, let your creative juices come alive.

Next we dance fire, the element of the solar plexus. What typifies fire better than Spanish flamenco music? Let yourself go passionately into the fire.

The fourth element is air that connects us to the heart chakra. Let your heart stir with the music from an opera love story. Connect with the sound and let your body speak in movement.

The music I've suggested is only intended to get you started. The possibilities are endless, let your imagination soar and play with it.

If you are dancing all the elements, a neat way to top it off is to tone the throat chakra. If the group is very shy, put on some background music to help them break through the selfconsciousness.

It never ceases to amaze me how quickly people loosen up and become like playful children, if you encourage them.

Laying on of Hands

Healing by laying on of hands has been around for a long time. Jesus did it and said what I can do so can you - and more! Healing methods can have different purposes or intentions. You can use laying on of hands to balance, to strengthen, to help heal physical injuries, for emotional release work and to foster spiritual healing. There are many methods out there and it's important to be clear about what your purpose is and what system you are using when working on a client.

I have chosen to present the biofield using chakra terms, and as you will see, all the flows derive naturally from the knowledge of chakras. For a clear presentation of the biofield and it's connection to physics, see the Handbook of SHEN by Richard Pavek (currently out of print).

On purpose, I have made no charts with hand positions. I want you to understand how the flows work, and be free to approach the client with what they need at this particular time.

Arm Flows

The natural flow of energy is from one hand to the other, up the arm, across the shoulders and down the other arm. The most powerful area for healing work is about the size of a quarter in the middle of your palm. Most people are right handed senders, making their right hand the sending hand and the left the receiving hand. Why some people are left handed senders I don't know. It has no connection with being right or left handed for writing etc. How do you know if you are a right or left handed sender? There is a test which I will share with you. If the results are inconclusive we generally assume the person is a right handed sender.

For the test you need to be at least two people. First the individual instructions. Sit in a chair. Rub your own palms together in a circular motion. Then sit with your arms resting comfortably, with your palms facing each other, not too far apart. Close your eyes and just focus your awareness on the quarter size surface at the center of your palms, can you feel anything? Keep breathing slowly and deeply while focusing on your palms, and just notice any sensations you become aware of. Try shifting the hands farther apart, then move them slowly back together again. Play with it until you get a sense of the energy between your hands. Now pair up with a partner. One of you hold your hands up in front of your chest with palms facing your partner. Your partner checks for which palm has most activity by holding first one hand in front of each palm, then the other hand in front of each palm. If you are more than two people in the group, switch partners and repeat the exercise. Don't share your results until everyone has completed the test.

If both hands seem equally active assume you are a right hand sender. After you've worked with the biofield awhile you may want to get retested, as your flows get stronger the more of this work that you do.

The flow through the arms is more like a pipe than a string, imagine a flexible pipe coming in your left palm, going up your left arm, continuing across your shoulders and down the right arm and out the right palm, a continuous circuit. This is the flow that you work with in laying on of hands. (Some other systems send from both hands, or transmit symbols or direct the energy.)

Arm flows are used for breaking up tension and for relaxation. They also enable held emotion connected to tension in the arms to release, and also have an effect on helping the throat open. Fairly often work on the hands bring up strong emotional memories from early childhood where a parent/adult has been holding the hand.

Spine Flows

The flow up the spine starts at the root or the tailbone and travels up the spine to the top of the head, or crown and beyond. It also flows from the root along the spine, then up to the front center of each chakra.

Spine flows relax body tension, but are primarily used for integration at the end of a session. Integrating flows from root to center(s) worked on, from root to sacral, and root to crown will help the client ground and center at the end of a session.

Peripheral Flows

Just like the arms have a directional flow, so do the legs and torso. The flow comes in the right foot, moves up the right leg, up the right side of the torso to the shoulder, follows the outside of the head around the top and then back down the left side, from the left shoulder down the side of the body continuing down the left leg and out the left foot where the flow loops around to connect with the inflow to the right foot. Again the flow is like a pipe the full cross section of the leg and about the same width through the torso. The flow is within the torso except around the head and below the feet.

Peripheral flows are used for relaxation, usually at the beginning of a session. Long peripherals, where your sending and receiving hands are stretched far apart as in from foot to shoulder, can be used for integration at the end of a session.

Rotary Flows

In addition to the straight pipe component of the arm and peripheral flows, there is a rotary component as well. If a person is laying on their back and you are standing at their feet looking toward their head, the rotary flow is counterclockwise up the right leg and clockwise down the left leg. Imagine a slinky or spiral moving up the right leg and up around the head and down the left side of the torso and leg. The arms also have a rotary flow, here you need to pay attention to if the person is a right or left handed sender. Assuming they are a right handed sender, the rotation looking up the left arm is counterclockwise, looking at it coming out the right hand it's clockwise. When the pipe flow is going away from where you are looking, it's counterclockwise, when coming toward you it's clockwise.

Rotary flows are used for relaxation and to break up tension.

Chakra Flows

Each chakra is like a fountain that comes out the front of the body. The chakra flow returns at the sides of the body, joining the rotary flows, and continuing along the back to the center of the spine. The return flows intersect between each chakra, also known as rearward lines. Imagining the chakra flows like a donut can be helpful.

Chakra flows are used for specific emotions and qualities the client has brought to the surface. The return flows to the side assist in emotional release. The return flows from the side of the torso to the center of the spine are used for back pain and injuries.

Transverses

Another useful flow is the transverse, which simply means across, for example a flow across a joint like the knees or elbows, or across the torso.

Transverses are used for breaking up tension and for physical relaxation.

Energy Bodies and Aura Work

The biofield not only permeates the physical body, but also extends out into the aura. Most of the time we work with our hands on the body, but there are several reasons to work in the aura. The biofield consists of several energy bodies: the physical, supra-physical, emotional, causal, mental and subconscious. Each of these bodies are found within the physical body, but also extend out into the aura. The physical energy body is contained within the actual body. The supra-physical extends just a little outside of the flesh and blood body. The emotional extends a little farther, then a little bit farther is the edge of the causal body, even further is the boundary of the mental body and farthest out is the edge of the subconscious body.

Energy Bodies Exercise

To get familiar with the energy bodies here is a group exercise. Warm up by rubbing your palms in a circular motion and feeling the energy ball between your hands. Have one person stand in the middle of the group. The rest of you stand in a circle of 3 - 4 meters diameter. Hold your palms up in front of you facing the middle person. Say to yourself, show me the edge of their subconscious body, gently feel their aura until you get a sense of that boundary. With practice, most people will get a sensation in the palm of their hands. Then ask to be shown the edge of their mental body, then the causal, emotional and supra-physical bodies in turn.

The name of the bodies give us clues to what they contain. The physical and supra-physical energy bodies work with physical issues. The emotional energy body is where we store the emotions. The causal body holds our karmic issues and deals with cause and effect. The mental body holds our beliefs and mental "programs". The subconscious body holds our memories and deepest motivations. The energy bodies are not separate, they interact and affect each other. The chakras exist in all the energy bodies.

When the material being worked on is deep or is difficult to chug loose it may be time to work in the aura. The energy flows naturally extend outside the body, so the same directional principles apply as when working directly on the physical body. I had some deeply held material surface and release recently when my Kairos therapist worked in the energy bodies outside my physical body. Generally you would start closest to the physical body and work your way out.

Equipment Needed

To work with a client with laying on of hands, you need some tools beside your hands to make the work flow smoothly. Start with a regular table, about 70 cm wide and 185 - 200 cm long. A 60 cm wide massage table works well too. On top, place a sunbed or camping cot of approximately the same dimensions and secure with bungee cords. If you are using a massage table, place wooden slats under the cot legs to protect the soft surface. For yourself, an adjustable office chair or stool on wheels. Normally the client lays fully clothed, face up on the cot. Put a small pillow under their head, and a larger pillow or roll under their knees to take the strain off the lower back. For supporting your arms while working on the client you'll need a couple of small pillows, rolled up towels, or foam cushions. You can place a blanket or thin foam pad on the bottom table for a softer working surface. I also place a blanket under the client, and cover with a sheet, to soften the feel of the camping cot. It's easier to wash sheets than blankets! Since I am in a nordic climate, I also cover the client with a cotton blanket. Get something that isn't too bulky, you need to be able to tell where the clients body landmarks are under the blanket. Use pillowcases on the client's pillows. Change the bedding regularly. Your clients will appreciate it. There is nothing worse than getting on a treatment table that isn't clean!

When working on a client make sure you are comfortable, you don't want to strain yourself. Breathe normally into your belly. Keep your spine straight and relax your body. The client's biofield is sensitive, let your hands approach the client softly, rest your hands lightly on their body where appropriate, and let your movements be fluid as you shift hand positions. Remember to remove hands gently.

For best results, ask your Higher Self to guide you to do what is for the highest good of your client.

Unfinished Business

Why do some events continue to haunt us lifetime after lifetime? Why do other events not affect us at all? Why does a group of people experiencing the same event have such different reactions? How can we change our habitual responses? Why is it that under stress, we respond from the part of us that is least functioning, acting like two year olds with a temper tantrum? These questions, and more, is what I'll attempt to answer in this chapter. We'll also talk about how to clear up this unfinished business.

To illustrate that the event need not be a huge trauma, although it can be, I'll use an example from my own life. I was in third or fourth grade, and our school was to participate in a sports competition. In the tryouts I was chosen to represent our class in the 60 yard dash. We arrive at the competition and I prepare for my race. We are off and running, I'm out front and my whole class is cheering me on, I look up and see this string tied across the goal line - I didn't know what to do, so I slowed down, and someone else won the race. My classmates asked me, why did you slow down, you were winning. I was too embarrassed to admit I didn't know what to do. I didn't know it was just a string of yarn that would break when you ran through it. Nobody had thought to explain it ahead of time. To help you understand the situation, this was in 1960 or '61, and we didn't yet have television, so I had never seen a real race. If I had, I would have known about the string they tie across the goal line, and how to break through it. This seemingly minor event affected my whole life, until it cleared in therapy. When I encountered an obstacle in my path, I would back off and not know how to "cross the finish line". If I wasn't given the information I needed to do a job, I would become livid (in other words angry). I was obsessed with making sure others got all the information they needed. Until it came up in therapy, I had not thought about the event since it happened, nor did I have any idea that I wasn't functioning as well as I could. The memory came during a therapy course and I totally relived the event on the table. It wasn't just a movie in my head, I felt everything I had felt back then, but had repressed deep into my body. Just remembering an event won't clear it. It's only when you allow yourself to totally feel and know yourself in the event and own the choices you made, that it can clear.

__To clear an event, you need to remember it, feel all the emotions associated with it, and recognize and own the choices you made at the time.__

Some events will come up a number of times in therapy, until it clears. I look at it like it's several layers of emotions and realizations that have to be worked through. If an event keeps coming up again and again, there is some component of it that isn't finished.

It wasn't until I recognized I had a choice to move with my parents to the United States or stay in Sweden at age fourteen, and realized the impact of the choice I made, that in choosing to stay with my family, I gave up myself. That's when the event cleared. It was a very painful realization, but it cleared out a lot of confusion, anger and blame.

When an event has cleared, it no longer has an emotional charge, and forgiveness comes automatically. You no longer have a need to talk about it.

It's amazing how something that has been a big trauma in your life suddenly completes. It's still a memory, but the emotions are basically neutral and it isn't important to talk about it anymore. You may even forget how you were before, not noticing the cage is gone.

When we repress our emotions during an event, it stays in our bodies until we go back and fully feel all the emotions and own our choices. If the event is traumatic, the body goes into shock, the root shuts down and with it all our emotions are repressed. This is natures way of keeping us sane. If we were to feel all the emotions at the time of the trauma, we wouldn't be able to cope with them. It's too overwhelming, so nature makes you go numb. But the emotions are still there, in your body, waiting for an opportunity to surface. It's like you had a sending beacon inside of you that attracts situations with similar emotional content, causing you to react in the same way as the original event. It does this for the purpose of tearing open the wound so you can heal it. And when you are triggered, your response goes on autopilot, and all of a sudden you behave like a two year old with a temper tantrum. If your reaction is out of proportion to the present circumstances, you can be sure an old emotional wound has been triggered. And it doesn't even need to be from this lifetime, it can be from before you were born or from a lifetime several thousand years ago.

Similar events form a string of emotional memories. Clear the first event, and the rest will follow.

0-0-0-0-0-0-0-0-0

I had a very vivid illustration of this principle during a therapy session. I was experiencing a pain in my left thumb, where I had been kicked by a horse (a stallion to be exact) in my youth. During the session I experienced a whole string of memories of former boyfriends who had "kicked me" in an emotional sense. The physical injury of being kicked by a stallion connected to emotional memories of being "kicked" by human stallions.

Breaking up Tension

To start to access our emotional memories, we need to break up the tension in our bodies. The tension holds the emotion prisoner and the buried emotion retains the physical tension. So starting with the physical is a way to access the buried emotions. This is also why we have such resistance to starting to exercise - some part of us knows unpleasant stuff can come up, that we've so carefully tucked away deep inside our bodies.

In the biofield chapter we covered breath and movement, sound, dance and laying on of hands as techniques to break up physical tension. Getting massage is another wonderful technique for breaking up physical tension. I personally prefer the Hawaiian lomi-lomi massage because it is so gentle and effective in loosening physical and emotional armoring as well as stimulating the natural life energy.

Some people are under chronic physical tension due to structural causes. One leg may be shorter than the other one, a hip may be dislocated, or there is some other structural misalignment. Finding ways to ease the effects of the chronic tension will help greatly in getting to the deeper layers. People under chronic physical tension generally need more work just to keep the tension stress at bay.

I believe each body has it's own optimal set of exercises - and it is up to each one of us to find that combination. Whether it's walks in nature, swimming, running, yoga, tai chi, chi kung, bicycling, aerobics, strength training or horseback riding. The possibilities are many, and the combinations vary. Keep trying and you will eventually find what works for you. It's normal to be more tired in the beginning. Don't worry, this will pass. Before you start any new exercise regimen it's smart to check with your physician.

We need three different types of exercise - stretching to keep us supple, aerobic activity to keep our hearts healthy, and strength training to keep our bones strong and muscles in trim. If it's difficult for you to get going, starting with strength training will actually help boost your energy, so you'll feel like doing aerobic type of activity. I've also found the movement and breath exercises great for overcoming resistance.

Natural light and fresh air are important for our well being, so try to make some of your activities outdoor ones.

If you aren't doing any exercise now, give yourself permission to start slow. It's better to take a walk once a week than not at all, and it's ok if they are short. Give yourself a pat on the back for having started, in time you can expand your program. It's so easy for us humans to get over ambitious, and when we can't live up to our unrealistic expectations, we give up. Less is more, in some cases.

Personally, I like videos better than going to a gym. For strength training made simple check out Strong Women Stay Young, it's available both as a book and video, put together by Miriam E. Nelson, PhD. For strengthening other muscles to take the load off your back, I recommend Callanetics by Callan Pinckney. I've already mentioned Movement and Breath Exercises for Personal Presence by Jane Hundley and The Art of Breathing - Chi Yi by Nancy Zi. For aerobics I like Linda Evans A New You.

Experiencing Emotions

In the last chapter we talked about starting to break up physical and emotional tension. So what should you do when an emotion comes up? Just be with it. If tears come, let them. Don't run to the refrigerator to find some "comfort" food to stop the feeling. Don't get on the phone to talk to your friends. Don't do anything. Just relax, and let yourself feel. There is no special breathing technique, just let your body bring up what you've been trying not to feel for a long time. Will it be unpleasant? Probably, but when you've felt the emotion fully, on the other side is peace, so it's worth going through. Don't you want to be rid of all this unfinished business you've been carrying around for eons? Of course you do. To fully feel an emotion, relax and soften, surrender to the feeling, let it swallow you up. Perhaps you are only aware of a physical sensation, just focus your awareness on that physical sensation, it will shift when it's ready.

What is the difference between experiencing and expressing an emotion? Expressing an emotion can be screaming, pounding pillows, stamping feet or talking about them. Unfortunately, this does not release the emotion, it only expresses it. To scream you have to tense your muscles, and even though you will get temporary relief, you haven't released the emotion. To release the emotion, you need to relax into the emotion and fully feel it. If you focus on softening and imagining yourself falling into the emotion, it's easier to let go.

How do we avoid our emotions? We avoid our emotions by talking excessively, by expressing instead of experiencing the emotion, by trying to analyze the emotion, by thinking about everything but what is going on with the body right now and by going to sleep. Or not wanting to go where our body leads us, trying to stay in control. Not being in our bodies - at one time it was too painful, so you fled your body, it's now become an unconscious response. To get back into the body takes practice but in time you'll be fully here and now.

It's time to introduce some more exercises. Both are good preparation for therapy and for use between sessions. The first one is to practice following the body sensations and staying with them until they dissolve, just like you would on the therapy table. The second one is more directed in that you fall through emotions layer by layer until you get to your source.

Become Aware

Turn off the phone and put up your do not disturb sign. Lay down in a comfortable place. Start by closing your eyes and taking a few slow deep breaths. Each time you breathe in, become aware of what you notice. It may be a sound outside, it may be an itch in your left thumb, it could be a thought "did I remember to turn off the phone?" or it could be a feeling like happiness. Stay present, just notice with each breath what you are aware of. If a sensation gets stronger, let it. If a thought persists, just let it, just keep noticing with each breath what you are aware of. If you space out, don't worry, it's normal, just return to being present with your body, thoughts and sensations. If images come up, don't try to analyze them, just be with them. Do this exercise as often and as long as you like. As you progress with this exercise you can let go of focusing with each breath, just stay present with whatever is going on, if your attention wanders, bring yourself back gently.

Emotions to Source

Make sure you are comfortable, either recline in a chair or lay down. Close your eyes. Take a few slow deep breaths and relax, let go. Ask yourself, what am I aware of right now - where in my physical body do I feel a sensation - describe it out loud - and put a name on the emotion you are feeling - now breathe into the emotion, feel it fully in your body, stay with it for 30 seconds up to 3 minutes - then fall through to the next layer of emotion, just let yourself fall and let go - then repeat the step - Ask yourself, what am I aware of right now - where in my physical body do I feel a sensation - describe it out loud - and put a name on the emotion you are feeling - now breathe into the emotion, feel it fully in your body, stay with it for 30 seconds up to 3 minutes - then fall through to the next layer of emotion - continue until you get to your Source, you'll know it when you get there, it's the place beyond time and space, that which some people call God. This is the center of your Self. Stay with your Source as long as you want. Then come back softly to here and now, open your eyes and stretch. With practice, you can add asking if there is a memory associated with each layer.

If you aren't used to feeling, these exercises may be difficult at first. Just being still and being with yourself may be a challenge, do what you can each time, and pat yourself on the back for having taken time out for yourself.

Emotions come disguised as physical sensations or mental chatter. The hungry feeling in the pit of your stomach may hide a deep longing for security. Underneath the painful knees may be a deep grief, or it could be something else, such as anger. Emotions reside not only in the chakras, but also in other parts of our bodies. More about this in the next chapter on where to work?.

Where to Work?

In this chapter I'll try to help you sort out where to work when doing laying on of hands. There are no set rules. Listening to your intuition is a very good tool. Understanding the structure of tension and emotional contraction is another. We need both logical structure and intuitive flow. Paying attention to what you feel in your own body may be an indication of your own stuff or a clue to what your partner needs worked on. Check it out before you assume it's their stuff. It takes time to get familiar with our own signals, and I've experienced that they can change over time as I change.

Most therapists take a client history. It tells them where the mines may be buried and gives them a place to start. It also tells them when to take on a client and when to refer them to someone else. Before you start working on someone you'll want to know enough of their history to be able to decide - if their deepest stuff comes up, can I help them through it? If not, refer them to a professional that can help them.

Taking a client history tells you where the mines may be buried

Client History

What do you need to know? Aside from their *name and address*, here are some suggested questions to ask:

What do you want help with? You want to make sure objectives are clear and also attainable.

What is going on in your life right now? Look for the metaphors in the current life situation. If they are job hunting without success, ask how it feels. Perhaps it brings up feelings of not being loved or not being acknowledged. Ask how it feels to not be chosen. Does it bring up survival issues? Have they felt this way before? Have they been in a similar situation, metaphorically?

Have you had a medical check for condition you want help with? If someone comes complaining of heart pain, and the cause is for example clogged arteries, they need to see a medical doctor. If the physical shows a healthy heart, then the cause may well be emotional and you could help them.

Medications you are taking and why? Some medications suppress emotions and laying on of hands may have limited effect. This question also tells you more of what they are carrying in their bodies. As emotions release, the medication strength and frequency may need to be changed - only their physician can determine this!

Other practitioners you are seeing and why? Tells you more of their state of affairs.

Major illnesses, surgeries, accidents, traumas? Gives clues of where in their bodies trauma is stored. Also used for interview purposes to access memory/emotion.

Major events in your life? Other events such as births, deaths, marriage, divorce, job changes, moves may or may not impact a person greatly. Explore the effect of major life changes, be curious and ask lots of questions. You never know what is buried until you start digging.

Other events that have affected you? Some seemingly minor events can end up affecting our whole lives.

Have you ever hit another person? I personally don't work with clients who have a history of being physically abusive. Unless you are a trained therapist that knows how to deal with this I recommend you don't either.

Have you ever attempted suicide? What stopped you? How would you deal with it if difficult memories surface in therapy? Unless you are a trained therapist who knows how to work with suicidal clients, you should not put your hands on this person. Laying on of hands may seem innocuous, but is in fact an incredibly powerful tool. My mentor used to do demos when giving talks, but stopped after demoing a peripheral brought the subjects abuse memories right up. Luckily the subject was already a client and my mentor could complete the process. You never know what is going to come up when you start working on someone.

Have you been diagnosed or hospitalized for psychiatric illness? Unless you are a skilled therapist with knowledge of how to work with psychiatric illness, leave this one to the professionals.

Do you have a support system of friends you can call on if difficult emotions arise during therapy? It's very important that your client has a support system. If they don't have it, they need to start on building that first.

May I discuss your case with your other practitioners and with my mentor? It's important to respect client confidentiality and get their permission.

While on the subject of precautions, you do not want to work on someone who's just been stung by a bee or other poisonous bites - you do not want to spread the poison in the body. Do not work on clients with blood clots as you may dislodge the clot and cause greater problems.

Should you keep detailed records of your clients sessions? It depends. I've gone back and forth on this. At times, it's helpful to have a lot of data. Filling out a long intake form is daunting to a lot of people. Some clients get worried about confidentiality when you write everything down. Personally, I find that trying to write down my observations gets in the way of being present with the client here and now. My current strategy is to either ask some questions before they come in or make the first session a talk only session. When clients come for intensives from farther away, you need to probe some of the deeper questions. You wouldn't want someone to arrive for a weeklong intensive only to discover they are actively suicidal or have some other issues that aren't appropriate for you to work on.

We've covered earlier how unfinished business stays in our bodies until the emotions and memories have cleared and we have owned the choices we made at the time. But where in our bodies do we store unfinished business?

Emotions are generally stored in chakras, but emotional release can occur anywhere in the body. Let's start with what we carry in each chakra, or what it represents.

Chakra Qualities and Emotions

Root - Connects us to earth and keeps us grounded. Affected when we move house, being uprooted, shuts down with major trauma and shock, deep grief, terror, horror, death, fear.

Sacral - Center of self, creativity, sexuality, self confidence, shame, guilt, self-loathing/hate, war, peace, sacred, self-love.

Solar Plexus - fear, anger, power, excitement, humor, boredom, anxiety, irritation, will to live, life mission.

Heart - love, sadness, grief, awe, reverence, remorse, hatred of another.

Throat - self expression, communication.

Brow - intuition, clairvoyance.

Crown - connection to spirit.

Any closed down chakra can be cause of low physical energy. My own chronic fatigue lifted when I fully experienced the intense anger I'd held in my solar plexus.

A word about fear. It can suffuse the entire biofield and seems to anchor itself at the location of the physical trauma.

A general rule for working with the chakras is to do ring rearwards to loosen and break up the tension, then do frontward to release emotion. If emotion is already flowing, go straight to the frontward flow. However, if your hands are already placed and emotion starts flowing - stay put - and do not move on until the emotion has released. Unless emotion is flowing, stay in each hand position until the energy comes through. To start with until you get a feel for when the energy has gone through, you can hold each position for three minutes.

OK, so the emotions and memories are stored in the body. What's this about breaking up tension? When we contract around an emotion, the physical body gets tight and tense. When we are nervous we can't eat, the chest gets tight when we feel grief making it hard to breathe, the solar plexus gets tense when we are afraid, we say my stomach is in a knot, and so on. We tense up around physical injuries and pain and this tension translates radially out through our body. Similarly, the knot in the stomach radiates out and affects the rest of the body and nearby organs.

If someone has a lot of tension in their bodies, it may take awhile to break through to the underlying emotional layers. Doing cross rearwards at the centers can break through a lot of tension. By cross rearwards I mean placing the sending hand for example at the sternum, which is on the heart/throat (HT) rearward line, and the receiving hand underneath the body on a line with the xiphoid (vee of ribcage), which is on the solar plexus/heart (SPH) line. With root trauma, you may need to work the legs and do extensive rearwards all around the body before the shock releases. When the shock lets go, the client can start to feel.

For deeper trauma, working with the extended flows in the aura may be needed to unravel all the threads. It's as if the tension is so great it can't be contained within the physical body. This seems to be especially true for older trauma, those hurts we've carried for a long time and buried deep within our cells. These memories rarely surface at the beginning of therapy, but at a much later stage. My own experience is that they surface when I have someone working on me that I know I can trust and that isn't going to wimp out when the really "good" stuff comes up.

It takes time to develop that kind of relationship between client and therapist or between trading colleagues.

With injuries, you'll need to work both the physical trauma location as well as the associated emotions, and they could be several, so it may take a few sessions to get through.

Observation

A few words about observing the client. While you are doing the interview, you may notice that your client's facial expression changes, the tone of voice goes flat or she chokes up etc. These are indications that emotions are percolating. When you put the client on the table, take a moment to observe the breathing - is it shallow or full, does the breath go into the entire torso or just parts. Where does the breath not go - this is an indication of held tension. What is the client's facial expression? As the session progresses, the client's journey may wander far from where the interview started. As a therapist you need to follow where the client takes you. In the beginning, it's impossible to take in all the information. If you pick focus areas to practice on it's easier. For a couple of weeks, just focus on observing breathing. Another few weeks pay attention to posture and body language. Then do facial expression, and so on. You will get a sense of which clues are your best tools - use them. Make your style your own.

Contrary to what many complementary therapies claim, there are no miracle cures. It can take time to put Humpty Dumpty back together again, especially if your client has a lot of physical tension, is in their head or out of touch with their bodies and emotions. However, traditional talk therapy generally takes a lot longer and may never get as deep as the methods described in this book.

Next we'll talk about how to evoke the emotions.

Evoking Emotions

If you look at this like a treasure hunt, it makes it easier and more fun. Earlier we covered interview questions to ask clients before they get on the table. You never know which question, or method, is going to get results, and the emotion probably won't come pouring out. It will need some nudging and encouragement to start flowing. Most of us are used to talking right over the emotion, and it takes practice to notice that moment when something significant is percolating just beneath the surface. Encourage the client to pause the stream of words, and just notice what they are feeling. It's easy to get caught up in the story and miss the emotion point, but with practice it gets easier. When emotion surfaces, encourage the client to stay with the feeling and put them on the table. Go straight to the emotion centre that is up. Be aware that tears can be sadness (heart), fear (solar plexus), shame (sacral) or deep grief (root).

Ask Questions

To evoke emotion let yourself be curious, ask them *tell me more ... have you felt this way before?... how did those around you react?* etc, there are a thousand questions you can ask. If some illogical thought pops into your head, ask that question too. Some people get pictures to guide them in the interviewing, others experience physical sensations, or just get a sense. I get a lot of information when I put my hands on the clients body, that's what speaks to me. Start to notice how you get your clues, and work to develop your very own style.

From the interview questions, you can take any event and dig deeper for information, remember that you are looking for the emotions present. What was it like to be left in the hospital? What was going on in your family around the time of your first migraine? You will be amazed at what people start to remember - Oh yeah, that's when my dog died. And how was that for you? Just keep following the thread that unravels and just keep digging for clues. Being a therapist is a lot like being a detective. My favorite massage therapist was like a bloodhound *what treasure have we buried here?* she would say as she probed a tender spot.

Coaching

To coach the client into emotion, use the situation they've talked about. Make the instruction simple and direct, for example *take yourself back to when you were standing at your mother's grave.* Timing and appropriate use of coaching takes practice and at times it will seem to have the opposite effect. Don't worry, you will put your foot in the mouth and really blow it occasionally, but that's how you learn. To risk making a fool of yourself is part of the process.

Drawing

Asking the client to paint or draw the situation or feeling is another method to evoke emotion. Ask the client to talk about the picture, what it means to them. A picture is worth a thousand words they say. Color crayons are just fine, it's not about creating masterpieces, but about accessing what is hidden inside. Just asking someone to draw can bring up memories of school - both pleasant and not. The client will probably need some guidance to get started, especially if they are not used to this kind of process work. The drawing doesn't have to look like anything, it can be colors, blobs, lines etc. For some people this process works well, for others not.

Awareness

Explore each client's possible keys to unlock their emotional treasures. Use the awareness exercises from the first chapter to help the client get in touch with their inner self. For many it takes practice to become aware of their feelings, they've gotten so used to skimming over them and pretending they are not there.

Storytelling

Telling a story, verbally or in writing, can be a doorway to emotion. And telling the story, especially in abuse cases, is an important part of the healing process. Telling our story to a group of supportive listeners can be very cathartic. Either tell the story spontaneously, or write it out then read it out loud to the group. It can be scary to start writing on our own, it's the buried emotions we are afraid to feel, because they are so strong. It's not unusual to want to avoid the pain, so don't be surprised if you have a hard time sitting down to get the writing done. Make an agreement with yourself that you are just going to sit there until you've finished your task, until you've sausaged your way through it. Running to the refrigerator, sorting paper clips, cleaning closets at this point are all avoidance techniques. Agree with yourself to just do it. And let the tears flow if they come, it's ok if your paper gets all spotted. Isn't it time to let it out, you've carried the pain long enough.

Sharing

Sharing is another technique used in group settings. As one person shares the group listens. Be present to what the person is saying, or not saying, pay attention to body language and other clues you may pick up. The person sharing needs to focus on what is going on right then and there, what they are feeling. So often sharing gets into a storytelling of what they ate and how they slept and all the details of their dreams and its an awful lot of information that unfortunately doesn't get to the heart of the matter. Dreams can reveal a lot if you focus on the emotion(s) present or what the dream represents. In sharing there is a fine line between letting people talk enough so they feel heard, and keeping it focused so the emotional material surfaces. In groups I like to vary the sharings - one word to describe present state, do an exercise, pick a theme such as "my most embarrassing moment" or "what scares me most", draw, do a dance, or story telling. Keep it varied. Some long and some short.

Silence

Silence is yet another technique, sit long enough, or put client on table, and something will surface. In modern times we are so used to constant noise and activity that silence can be a great doorway into emotion.

Regression

This chapter wouldn't be complete without doing a regression exercise. This exercise you can do either individually or with a group. First get clear on the issue you want to focus on. Then get comfortable, take a few deep breaths, all the way down into the belly, relax and let the day go, let yourself surrender to the process. We are now going to take a journey back to the origin of the issue you've chosen to focus on. Let yourself become aware of your body, let it relax body part by body part, starting at the feet. Let your feet relax and notice how they get heavier and heavier. Let your legs go, feel how heavy they are. Let your buttocks go, relax and go even deeper. Let your belly go, feel it relax and go soft. Let your ribcage relax, feel it expand, letting in more air, letting in more of you. Let your shoulders relax and soften. Let go of the burdens you carry. Just let go. Let your back relax, feel the tingle up and down the spine as your back lets go. Now let your neck and shoulders relax and feel the relaxation flow down your arms all the way out through your fingertips. Sigh, let yourself go. Feel your scalp and head relax, let your jaws drop and feel your eyes sink deeper as you sink deeper and deeper.

Now imagine yourself in a tunnel, you are surrounded by color. First you are moving through the red section, let the red surround you and permeate you, take in all the red that you need ... next the tunnel goes orange, breathe in all the orange you can muster, feel yourself go deeper into orange ... and the tunnel becomes yellow, a bright yellow, taste it and see it all around you and through you ... and the tunnel becomes green, soo green, you are completely surrounded by green and it permeates you and all your senses ... now the tunnel becomes pink, it shimmers and you sink into this pink cloud ... moving along it turns blue, sapphire blue, let yourself hear the tones of sapphire blue, let it permeate you ... and moving into indigo, a midnight blue, let the indigo connect you with your intuition, see it all around and through you ... and the tunnel is purple, and you become one with the purple and sink even deeper.

Now focus on the issue you want to work on, the one that it's time to let go of. Let yourself go back to the first time to the origin of this issue (if you are working with an individual, repeat the exact issue to get the client totally focused on it). Imagine yourself magically transported across time and feel yourself moving back to the origin of your current issue. Now you are there, at the origin. Look down at your feet, what are you wearing? (Pause after each question, allow plenty of time for the material to surface. If working with an individual, have them answer the questions, again give them plenty of time). Are you aware of any sounds or smells? Are there other people there? What are they wearing? Who are they? Do you know them in this life? Where are you? What year is it? What is your name? Are you a man or a woman? How old are you? What is going on? Let yourself feel the situation. (you may need to vary the questions, depending on what the answers are - you may need to coach the client to get a hold of the situation, be there as a guide for them - let your intuition help you - these scripts are only intended as a starting point, to use as a guide). Keep asking questions until the process feels complete. If emotions come up, encourage the completion of them, *just let yourself feel, let the feeling get stronger, let yourself go deeper into that feeling* then move on once the emotions have percolated through. When the issue feels exhausted, say: now it's time to return to normal waking consciousness. I will count from one to five and on five you will open your eyes fully refreshed, awake and alert. One, starting to come back. Two, take a deep breath. Three, feel your fingers and toes. Four, more and more awake. Five, open your eyes. Stretch and come back to here and now.

Take some time to talk about the journey. If more emotion comes up, pause and encourage *let yourself be with that* then move on. In regressions, as with any therapy process, the important thing for the client to focus on is to allow themselves to fully experience all the emotions of the event, that's when it lets go. And when the realization drops in of the consequences of the choices made at the time of the event, that's when it's finished, and the need to talk about it disappears.

For some really great scripts of regressions for emotional and physical issues, get the book The Journey by Brandon Bays. When the book came out in Sweden my friend said this is what Eva does, but she uses different techniques. My way of describing the Journey process is that it's a combination of

Kairos/Shen and Hypnotherapy/NLP. The book is a fascinating read of how Brandon Bays healed a tumour the size of a football. Although she was an expert on NLP, this healing journey showed her that the key lay in releasing emotional hurts from the physical body.

When you are working with clients, I advise using scripts only as a starting point. Rarely does the client follow the script from a text. When you practice, focus on staying present with the client and explore the threads or emotions they bring up. Learning several different techniques to work with your clients will make you a better therapist.

A word about the difference in working individually and with a group. The group process is often experienced stronger, we set each other off and there is more energy in the room. But it depends on our issues. Sometimes an issue is more easily triggered in a group, other times it's the individual session that does it for us. Most of us need a mix of group and individual work to progress.

Change can occur very softly, very gently. It's not necessarily the big dramatic releases that effect the most change. It can be a very quiet realization that causes the most profound shift in our lives. God steps softly in our hearts.

Release and Integration

Therapy can help you release that which stands in your way to really be yourself. But you are the only one that can take the steps that bring you forward. I've seen many people get stuck in therapy and not really progress past a certain stage. I think they are afraid to let go, and have in some way become dependent on the therapist. One of my earliest teachers broke up a weekly group because she felt some of the members had become too dependent on the group. It was a great lesson in letting go. It helped us all move on, which is what we really needed. I've found that over time my teachers and therapists have changed and so do the people I trade with. This is normal progress.

Positive Experiences

Some of my biggest releases have come after I've had the chance to experience normal, or getting what I didn't get as the younger me. When I was laid up with a broken ankle last fall, I experienced for the first time in my life being totally taken care of. The home service came to help me in the morning with showering, getting dressed, doing the dishes etc. At midday they came again with a hot meal and dessert. My country store delivered other groceries and my friends showed up to help with housecleaning, laundry, garden chores etc. They came and kept me company, took me on outings and brought me books to read. It was one of the most rewarding experiences of my life. In contrast, my mother hadn't been able to be there for me as a baby. My grandmother fainted with some mysterious illness when I was 3 weeks old and stayed in bed for the next 3 or 4 months at our house. To top it off my grandfather also moved in with us, adding to my already overwrought mother's burden. The little baby, me, did not get all the care and attention she needed. I have had issues with abandonment, not feeling loved or wanted, my whole life. This, in turn, set me up for an abusive husband (long since ex) who seemed bent on destroying me.

It was in therapy sessions following the positive nurturing experience that the little baby could begin to heal. It was only after I had experienced what I had missed, that I could access the deep hurt and longing.

If there are issues of self worth or abandonment - and who doesn't experience them - just having a person who believes in you and supports you can have a profound effect on your healing. Never underestimate the power of love. In a study of successful entrepreneurs they all had at least one person who had believed in them and supported them unconditionally through the journey from idea to success.

Non-verbal Coaching

Another trigger for release is what we call non-verbal coaching. Holding someone's hand or touching their cheek like you would to comfort a child can be powerful doorways into release. When there are issues around love and self love, you can hold the client's hand on top of the heart or sacral chakra. When there is birth trauma you can do a root to crown flow while squeezing with a gentle pressure. When you use non-verbal coaching pay attention to your motivations and do it gently.

Tears and Pain

Did you know that there are many different ways to cry? And that some expressions of crying actually get in the way of you really experiencing the emotional pain. When a painful memory first surfaces, we may go through extreme sobbing, even cramping and our body contracts. We may make whiny sounds and other noise as our throat tightens up. As the experience deepens and you surrender to the next layer, let yourself soften and fall into the pain. Here the crying is quieter, however the pain may be more excruciating. Why is that? Well, as you soften, you are actually experiencing the emotion at a deeper level. Tensing up and making a lot of noise is not productive in the long run, if you really want to let go. To let go, you have to eventually go to that quiet place where the pain is and just be the pain. Here there may not even be any tears. When you've fully felt it, it lets go. You may be surprised at how soft and gentle that letting go can be.

Spitting Up

It doesn't happen often, but occasionally you get a client that spits up or vomits during a session. They may report feeling queasy before getting on the table or it may come up while you are working on them. Don't worry, queasiness is a normal reaction when the emotions held are strong or very deep. The body wants to get rid of the unpleasant feeling, so it vomits. Likewise, some clients develop irritable bowels, they let go that way. Keep a plastic lined wastebasket in your therapy room. You won't need it often, but you'll be glad you have it when the client all of a sudden announces *I feel sick*. Have them sit up and let it out, then lay them on their side. Give them water to drink to help rehydrate and help flush out the toxins. Keep working the session to help their body release and integrate what is there. Sometimes there is a memory of having been sick that has surfaced. Probe what was going on in their life at that time to access the deeper layers.

Movies

Emotions may not surface during a session, but come afterward. This is quite common in fact. Letting yourself just be with the emotions is all that is required. I find videos very helpful when I just need to cry. Put on a sniffle movie, snuggle down on the couch, box of Kleenex nearby, and let the tears flow. I also recommend this approach when you have family around that may not be totally understanding of the need to release emotion in conjunction with therapy. Just about anybody can be sympathetic if you cry during a romantic love story. They need not know that you are grieving your lost childhood or whatever.

Body Work

If you've gone through a big release it helps to integrate the changes in your body. Get a massage, go for a walk, or work out at the gym. This helps the energy move through and complete the release and anchors the new energy pathways in your body. If the shift has been a big one, work out carefully. As muscle tension relaxes, the way you carry yourself also shifts. Your hips may be looser, or you discover you walk different. Give your muscles a chance to get used to the new you.

Self Flows

There are a lot of flows you can do on yourself with laying on of hands. Go back and study the biofield flows and then experiment on yourself. I lay in bed and prop pillows around to make it easier on my hands and arms. For the hand that is behind the body I turn the palm facing away from the body.

There is less strain on my anatomy this way, however the flows take a little longer to go through. Teach your clients some basic self flows to help them complete releases and integrate sessions.

Session Length

So how long is an ideal session? It varies. If emotions are right on the surface, the session can be quite short. My shortest appointment time is 45 minute. For deeper stuff, longer sessions work better. It's not unusual for regressions to take 2 to 3 hours. Intensives of several hours per day over several days can be very productive. I recommend a maximum of 5 hours per day over 5 days, or a 25 hour intensive. More than that just gets exhausting for client and therapist and is unlikely to produce more results. Getting the client up for breaks and moving around in between sessions helps to keep the biofield activated.

Cutting Aka Chords

To help release our attachments to other people, to clear karmic ties and to clean up relationship threads we can use the following exercise from the Hawaiian Huna tradition. It's called cutting the aka chords. These chords are like threads that connect us to other people. Some of these connections are very healthy and loving, others rob us of energy and need to be cleared. Think of it as cleaning out the cobwebs in the biofield or like going through the etheric car wash.

Turn off distractions and get comfortable. Take a few deep breaths and focus your awareness inward. Ask your Higher Self to be present and guide you through this exercise. Now notice chords coming from other people into your body, some will be thin, others thick, some can even be chains. Ask your Higher Self to show you which ones are not for your highest good. Work with the threads of one person at a time. Take the threads one at a time, feel it, notice where it enters your body and how the thread feels and looks and who it is connected to. You can use any tools you like to remove the chord, your imagination is unlimited. It's important to remove all of the thread all the way down to the roots. As you pull the thread out and unravel it, let it return to it's source, the other person it's connected to. See their Higher Self with them and notice how they take back what belongs to them, not you. When all the threads have been returned to a person, thank them and see them dissolve into the light in an aura of love and forgiveness. Return to your own body and do a final cleanout and fill the area with light. If emotions surface while you do this exercise, pause, let the emotions flood your senses and move on when they feel complete. At the end of the exercise, spend some time basking in the light of your Higher Self and feel the new you sparkle and shine.

Writing

Other ways to integrate our experiences include writing our story or painting our emotions. Both methods help integrate as well as release and access new layers. If your therapy has been about a particular memory or time period in your life, simply write down your story. Tell it from beginning to end, include how you felt, how others around you reacted - or didn't react. Write about what you wished could have happened, what you would have done different if you had had other resources or skills. Write about what you have learned. Keep writing until you are empty. If you are part of a therapy group, ask if you can read your story out loud at the next meeting. Notice how it feels to be acknowledged, to tell your story and be heard. A note to the therapy group, focus your attention and really listen to the storyteller. Perhaps you have a reaction of your own to share.

Painting

Painting can be used in so many ways, to awaken emotions, to explore our consciousness and to release even more material. With clients who have difficulty verbalizing what they are feeling, painting can be an incredible tool for them to discover their inner worlds. In my early stages of therapy I painted like a madwoman, unleashing many years of suppression. I painted a weeping willow that really wept, a stomping foot, a tiger clawing red blood, a dragon spurting fire, a volcano erupting with rage, a graveyard full of black crosses and swords with blood spouting. My therapist was an artist so it was a natural way for her to work with me. Each session I'd bring my pictures and we'd go on from there. You don't need to be an artist, working with crayons or watercolors on paper is fine. Let go of the outcome and become the process.

God put a Dream in my Heart

Have you wondered if you have a life mission? Do you think about the quality of life? Do you feel that you spend your time on activities that have little or no meaning to you? Your soul has a purpose for your life and it is through our intuition we get impulses to change our life. Energetically, the matrix or pattern for your Life Mission resides in the center of the solar plexus chakra in the causal body.

The cornerstones of this process are to learn to communicate with your inner guidance, to reach clarity about what your gifts are and what you long to experience, to understand what stands in the way of your development and tools to take your dreams from idea to reality. Learn to work with your intuition and increase your creativity through some more meditative exercises.

What do I really want to do with my life?
What prevents me from doing it?
How do I create my heart's desire?

Understanding God's plan for our lives isn't always easy. Our true desires and values may be buried under layers of what we think we should want or what we think is our duty. The trick is to let go of reasoning mind for a moment. Let's do a group exercise:

Circle Method

The circle method starts with everyone sitting in a circle. Get comfortable in your chairs and let go of the day's worries and concerns. This exercise trains you to be present, to listen and to speak from your inner self. It works like this. Each person speaks in turn, I prefer going around the circle to the left or clockwise. The person whose turn it is sits quietly until compelled to speak, don't worry about what you are going to say, just speak as the words form. The words may come at once or take time, just let the process work through you. If no words come, just say pass and the turn goes to the next person. The rest of the group just listens, focus your attention completely on the person whose turn it is, you don't need to prepare what you are going to say, it'll come when it's your turn. Take one of the questions above as a focus and keep going until everyone says pass all the way around. When it is your turn, you may want to state the question out loud, then wait for your answers to bubble up from inside of you. You may be surprised at what comes out. Other good ways to prime the process is to start each sentence with *What I really want...* or *What I actually desire...* or *What I don't want...* or *Before I die I want to...* or

When I was a child I dreamed of... or *What stands in my way?* or *What do I need to resolve and who can help me with this?*

God's plan for each man transcends the limitation of the reasoning mind, and is always the square of life, containing health, wealth, love and perfect self-expression.
- Florence Scovel Shinn

The future is calling you, not the other way around. Or put differently *Before you call I shall answer*. On the spiritual plane there is no competition, because what you can do, no-one else can do.

Life is a treasure hunt, and it is up to us to hear the whispers, to pay attention to our dreams and to have the courage to follow up. We don't need to understand everything. When we listen in stillness, we may hear a whisper to follow a certain path. Stuart Wilde, one of my favorite authors, describes it as our Higher Self keeps sending the message "left dodo" but we keep stumbling along ignoring that voice, until we finally get it and try going left, and lo and behold, there's a whole gang waiting for you. "What took you so long!" they exclaim.

Before I moved to Paradis, I'd had a vision for years of a little house in the country surrounded by meadows and birch trees and water, with real seasons, especially winter. I kept seeking help to find my true path, and all the experts swept my vision aside and said, yes but what are you going to do for a living? You need to be practical. When I finally heeded my inner voice and went for the house in the country, I ended up in Paradis and my neighbors first words to me were "where have you been for all this time?"

What I have discovered is that we are given clues and if we follow that thread we'll end up with the rest. Follow the golden thread and let go of the rest. Just like Dorothy in the Wizard of Oz we progress when we

follow the yellow brick road

Clue Threads

Next we'll do a clue exercise. From one of the following areas

- work
- home
- relationships
- health

describe what you dream of, either in words or by drawing, color crayons are fine, we are not looking for a masterpiece, but attempting to get in touch with your inner dreams. What ends up manifesting in your life may not look exactly like your picture, but it will have the same feel.

Now that we've started to uncover your dreams it's appropriate to talk about fear. There are only two kinds of people - those who are afraid and don't do it and those who are afraid and do it anyway. I've found the following fear exercise quite helpful:

Writing Down the Fear

Fear Exercise in completing the thought.

Day 1: Write I am afraid of..., because then I get..., then... happens, then I feel..., and then...

continue to write your thoughts to completion

repeat I am afraid of... until you have emptied your fear thoughts.

Fold up the paper and hide it, just like you've done with your fears before.

Day 2: Take out the paper. Read through every word, embellish the text even more, write until you've emptied yourself to completion. Fold up the paper and hide it again.

Day 3: Take out the paper, read it out loud by yourself, or if it feels right, read it to the group. Tear up the paper and burn or throw it away.

Bringing the fears out into the open starts to dissolve them. When you do this exercise you will find that the same bottom line fear surfaces. This bottom line fear is connected to what Jane Hundley calls our BLT or Basic Limiting Thought. The opposite, or positive aspect of our BLT, is our Personal Truth. When we are present in our Personal Truth, we are our Life Mission. When I would do the above fear exercise, I would always end up at a bottom line fear of being abandoned. When I went through Jane's transformative workshop, it turned out my BLT is *I am not loved*, and my Personal Truth is *I am loved*. See how they connect?

Present-Future

Another good way to get in touch with our inner dreams and to get direction and help to move toward the future that is calling us, is the Present-Future exercise. Often what our conscious mind says to do is contrary to what our Higher Self has in mind for us. This exercise puts the Higher Self back in the driver's seat.

There are three elements to keep in mind while doing this exercise. They are mindfulness, gratitude and compassion, especially for ourselves. Say to yourself "I open myself to what is necessary and useful in taking these next steps in my process". Practice watchfulness - how can it happen? Get into a relaxed and meditative state, then imagine yourself in your circle of present life, see it on the floor in front of you, feel all the qualities. Observe who or what is in the circle, notice any feelings or themes in the present circle. Stay with the present circle until you have a clear sense of the now in your life. Then, close to the present circle picture another circle - your future circle, which contains the life you are moving into, the parts you want to draw to you. Observe the future circle, how does it feel, who is present, what are you doing? Sense what was in past life that you will leave behind. Some parts will be precise, others more diffuse, some will be nebulous qualities.

You can move back and forth between the circles, notice the difference, what is changing in your life. Then ask if there is any "homework" for you to do. Whatever you are given is your next step. Spirit rarely gives us the whole plan at once, but if we do the steps given to us, then we will be given the next step. This exercise excites your own life energy and helps you to draw the future to you. Do as much as is comfortable. The temptation may be to do it again without doing the homework - sorry, that isn't going to work.

I used this exercise a lot in getting to my house in the country. Some of the early homework was to clean out my closet, my body was very specific - no more high heeled shoes, no more business suits or tight clothes. Until I cleared out the closet, I couldn't move forward. So I packed up several thousand dollars worth of corporate clothing and donated to charity. Then I got instructions how to find my country house. As I would complete one step or homework assignment from the present-future exercise, I would go back in and do the exercise again, get the next step and so on. Part of the process is to trust that your Higher Self is guiding you for your highest good. Your reasoning or logical mind may not understand, and that's ok. But I think it's time we talked about common sense.

Common Sense

How do I know it's God's voice and not some aberration that is making itself heard? This is an important question and we humans need to learn and practice discernment.

When you go to a psychic, medium or channel the material is always affected by the instrument's belief system. Even a really clear channel is on their best days only 85% accurate. Why? Because the helpers on the other side are there to help us, not do the job for us. So they throw in inaccuracies because we are supposed to filter the information and take what rings true to ourselves. This strengthens our intuition and trust in ourselves. The ultimate goal for a good channel is to work themselves out of business so that you learn to connect with your Higher Self and get the information directly.

The Higher Self is the best source of advice for your highest good. The advisors that work through channels and mediums are just like any other advisors you consult, such as your friends, accountants or lawyers, only they have a different perspective. Earth-bound advisors know about the physical plane, what is involved in functioning as a human being on earth. Spirit entities may not have been on earth for a long time, so their perspective is different, and it's good to keep in mind that their expertise is the non-physical plane.

For ease of definition we talk of the conscious self, the unconscious or subconscious, and the superconscious or Higher Self. We are not really compartmentalized and the boundaries are fluid between these states of consciousness.

The conscious self is our everyday awareness, here and now. Our logical or reasoning mind hangs out at the conscious level. We use the conscious self to function in everyday life.

The subconscious is where we store our memories and beliefs, the seat of the inner child. If there is a conflict between the beliefs of the conscious and the subconscious, it is always the subconscious who "wins". The Hawaiian Hunas name their lower self, like a child, and connect with it to access the Higher Self.

The Higher Self is your spiritual connection, your true guidance, and it always wants what is for your highest good.

So when you get information in these exercises, how do you know it is your Higher Self that is speaking?

If it would harm another person, it is not the Higher Self.

If it is not ethical, it is not coming from your Higher Self.

If it decreases your life energy, it is not a directive from your Higher Self.

The ultimate responsibility for all your actions is your own, that you can never get away from. You can never abdicate responsibility for your life. The Higher Self is your guidance, here to help you, love you and assist you. The Higher Self is patient, loves you unconditionally, and never gets upset that you didn't get it - they just keep nudging you in their very gentle way.

Well, gentle is perhaps not always true. It starts with a gentle tap on the shoulder, then another, but if they keep nudging and nothing happens, they may get out the 2x4 and we finally pay attention - oh, were you talking to me?

I am human

I believe we are spiritual beings in human bodies, doing our best to develop here on earth, to learn the lessons that can only be learned here.

As a human, I make mistakes. I don't always follow the guidance of my Higher Self. Perhaps I don't understand what is best for me. Perhaps I don't agree and go ahead with my version of the truth with a capital T. Perhaps I'm pigheaded and don't want to listen to my Higher Self.

This is all normal and part of being human. Making mistakes is ok. If we haven't known failure, would we enjoy success? Learning from our mistakes is part of the plan. Does a child worry about getting it right the first time? Of course not, it just keeps trying and trying until they do. It's only us adults that think we have to be perfect.

The Higher Self guides, the human chooses. Making choices is also our responsibility. To not make a choice, or to postpone the decision, is also a choice. But remember, *you can't do it right, and you can't do it wrong. You can only be yourself.*

Grail

Perhaps it's appropriate to talk about the Grail next, or how to follow the flight of intuition and cross the chasm of no data. A good mantra is

I remember to surrender

which helps you find the courage to take the first step. To surrender means to turn it over to God, to let go of trying to force our way. The spiritual solution is always better, but rarely looks the way we had pictured. We too easily limit future possibilities by using past experience as a guideline.

I have felt for a long time that I was supposed to write a book. Well meaning friends have pointed out to me that I'm not an author, that I need to focus on reality, that I need to simplify my marketing, that it's too much etc etc. It's not that easy to just listen to that soft whisper and take the time to write. I had enough of my own doubts come up. Would anyone want to read it? Look at all the books already out there. Isn't my time better spent selling my services to the corporate sector, just focusing on massage and meditation? I didn't have a lot of enthusiasm for that. Well, I had finally got started on the book and I fell and broke my ankle! Now I had the peace to do the writing. God works in mysterious ways!

In writing the book, the important thing for me is to stay present to the process. The outcome may be a finished book, or not. It may or may not get published. It's my doing the writing that is important, the doing produces clarity. The goal may not be what I think it should be, but it's only in the doing that I will discover what the outcome is going to be. I grow and change through the process, I am the product.

I like to talk about the Grail using the movie Indiana Jones and the Last Crusade as an example. In it we learn that he who finds the Grail must face the final three challenges:

1. the Breath of God - only the penitent man will pass, the penitent man is humbled before God, kneels before God
2. the Word of God - only in the footsteps of God will he proceed, the name of God, Iehovah
3. the Path of God - only in the leap from the Lion's head will he prove his worth, it's a leap of faith, you must believe

The way I interpret this is that the first principle is to surrender to the will of Spirit and to let go of our personal will. The second principle tells us to walk in God's footsteps, that is to follow the path of God. Thirdly to take the leap of faith and cross the chasm of no data. If you haven't seen the movie, go rent it and observe as Harrison Ford gets to the edge of the cliff, a deep chasm is between him and the Knight with the Grail, you can't even see an opening in the opposing cliff wall, but he knows the Knight is there. There is only one thing to do. Pray and take the first step. As you watch the movie, you are sure that Harrison Ford is going to tumble down into that chasm and disappear forever. Not so, he puts a foot out, and magically, a walkway is formed under his foot and in the cliff opposite a doorway opens up. He walks across and sure enough there is the Knight and the Grail. So too must you take that leap of faith, you won't know what will happen until you do, but

God makes a way where there is no way

If you hesitate and aren't sure, ask yourself "if I don't take this step now, will I wonder for the rest of my life what would have happened if I had done it?". If the answer is yes, do it!

Some tidbits of wisdom:

Everything I need to know is revealed to me.
Everything I need comes to me.
- Louise Hay

Spirit doesn't care about convenience

You must be willing to risk to grow

In the willingness to surrender and let go of everything, you create the space for new growth

If you love something
set it free
if it comes back to you, it is yours
if it doesn't, it never was

The Grail quest can also be described as an initiation. There are again three elements:

1. Face fear
2. Go through test
3. Secret is revealed

By doing the very thing you are afraid of, you dissolve the fear. The trick is to hang in there long enough to come out the other side of the fear, that is the test. Then, and only then, will the secret be revealed. Sorry, there are no shortcuts.

Creating Change

When we finally discover that which is really important in our lives and start the journey to create our own Paradise, that's when all our old unfinished business comes up. The Path to Light goes through darkness. What do I need to deal with? How do I work through the old that stands in the way of my path forward? Circumstances in our lives open up old wounds so we can heal them. That's why therapy is so important.

Thinking about it in another way, we want to focus our energies like a laser *toward* what we want. In order to do that we have to clean house of all the *away* froms. Any time we say I don't want... we are dealing with an *away* item that takes energy from our *toward*.

Wedging Principle

To make it easier to create change in our lives, we can use the wedging principle. Let's take an easy example. Say you have a goal of meditating 20 minutes per day, and that at the moment you aren't doing any at all. Using the wedging principle you would start with 5 minutes per day. It gets you started, it establishes the habit and it's easier to find 5 minutes than 20 minutes. Once you have established the habit and the 5 minutes feel comfortable, you can expand it to 10 minutes, then 15 and finally to 20. This can take time, and that's ok. Voilà, you have wedged a new habit into your life.

Hara Line

Here's a good meditation practice to get you more aligned with your true self. It's called the Hara Line meditation. The Hara is the same as the Sacral chakra, just a different name from a different language. Sit in a chair with your back and spine straight and your feet resting comfortably on the floor. Close your eyes, take a few deep breaths to center yourself. If you need a little grounding, let yourself become aware of your feet resting on the floor, the feel of gravity in your body, how your buttocks and back contact the chair.

Now focus your awareness in the center of your sacral chakra, located inside your body, halfway between the navel and the top of the pubic bone. Concentrate your awareness on this point, stay there until you really feel it. You may get a sense of fiery heat in this point. Then drop a line straight down to the center core of the earth. Focus on the molten core of the earth like a point, stay there until you feel really connected, then shift to connecting the two points and strengthening the line between them.

Now move your attention to the soul point, located between the heart and the throat at the sternum, inside your body. As you focus on this point, you may become aware of your chest opening up and becoming lighter. Stay with this point for a while. Then go back and connect up all three points, the earth core, the sacral and the soul point.

Next move your awareness to a point about 3 feet (about 1 meter) above your head, your identity point. Focus on it until you feel it well. Then connect the line between all four points.

In the beginning it may be hard to sense all the points. Pretend as if you could feel them, eventually you will. It's what I call fake it 'til you make it, or make believe creates reality.

fake it 'til you make it
make believe creates reality

There is the story of the famous actor. It turns out he was a shy and pimply faced teenager. He pretended he was suave and debonaire in front of mirror, and one day he discovered he had become what he pretended.

My niece was playing that she was a writer in Japan, dressed up in her Grandmother's silk bathrobe with the typewriter in front of her. A few years later the family moved to Japan, making at least part of the pretend come true. She may be a writer yet, who knows?

So the principle is to see it as already done. We practice in our imagination, and eventually we become what we imagine. The same holds true for what we fear. We attract that too. *Be careful what you wish for you will surely get it* the saying goes.

We create from inside to outside. Be gentle with the new seed, nurture it in secret, let it grow strong before you share it with others, and then only with those directly affected. To talk about it with friends, relatives and acquaintances scatters the life force.

Affirmation with Subconscious Response

Here's another exercise to create change. It helps to surface what keeps us from creating what we want. Take four sheets of paper. Draw a line vertically down the middle of the paper, creating two columns. In the left you are going to write the same affirmation over and over on all four sheets of paper, or about 100 times. After each line, on the right, you will write the subconscious response that comes up. Say you want to make sure you follow your intuition, you could affirm *I follow my intuition.* So in the left column you write *I follow my intuition.*

Then in the right column you write the first response that comes into your head. The response may be *how do I know it's my intuition?* Then write *I follow my intuition* on the left, response is perhaps *not all the time.* Keep repeating affirmation, write response, keep going until all four pages are filled. You may be surprised at what comes up. If emotion surfaces, pause and be present with the sensation, soften into the emotion until it clears, then continue the exercise. You can do this exercise every day until the response column matches the affirmation column. For stubborn issues, get on the therapy table.

Discover a Different Way of Life

What is life about? We dream a dream... we manifest it... then we experience it... once we have fully experienced it, then what? We start over. It's time to dream another dream... etc

One way to change the way you live is to shift your focus. So often, we see all that isn't right with our lives and with our world. I'm very much reminded of this presently, as national elections in Sweden are only two weeks away. All that isn't functioning with the current system is up for debate and election promises. So it feels appropriate to talk about gratitude. The other evening, a Swedish actress talked on television about the angel Gabriel, who holds two bowls, one for prayer and one for thanks. It's easy to fill up the prayer bowl, but we need to also fill the gratitude bowl, so Gabriel can stay balanced.

Gratitude Journal

A Gratitude Journal is a nice way to do this. You can get a nice diary or just a plain spiralbound notebook will do. The important part is to write in it. Every night, before you go to sleep, you write in your journal at least three *I am grateful for...* Three isn't the limit, it's just to get you started. Gratitude helps to shift your focus and attention on what's good and gets your mind off problemsolving. Notice if you sleep differently and if you feel differently, you probably will. Your life may start changing in surprising ways.

Since starting my quest, I've changed the way I live. Most days I don't set an alarm, I let myself wake naturally, and the time I get up can vary a bit. I try to not schedule appointments early, as I like my mornings to myself. I get up, make some tea, do some yoga or other exercise, then I meditate. In my morning meditation I ask for guidance, what is important for me today. And I do my best to follow that intuitive approach, but I'm human and the reasoning mind gets carried away sometimes, I'm not perfect. If I was I'd have wings and not have a real physical body. My life functions much better when I live from the inside out. I usually go out for a walk in the woods sometime during the daylight hours, and I often lie down for a bit after lunch. My diet plan is to indulge myself and never miss a meal. Truly, if you indulge yourself without guilt you satisfy the craving, and it lets go of you.

In his book Tantra for the West, Marc Allen describes how he used to have a craving for donuts, but he never let himself eat as many as he wanted. So he decided to test his tantra philosophy on indulging his craving for donuts. Tantra simply means going through the experience, becoming one with it - not back off, hop over it or go around it. So he went into the donut place and ordered up a plate of donuts, and started in, savoring each one. He kept eating and really tasting and enjoying each one until he felt satisfied, and quite full and a bit weird from all the sugar. Then he ate two more, just to be sure. Ok, he felt a bit sick afterwards, but the craving went away. Be sensible, if you are diabetic or have other medical problems, this is not the exercise for you.

It Feels Right

At one of my groups a participant asked *How do I know if it's right for me?* So we did an exercise on when it feels right and when it feels wrong. Simply get into a meditative state then ask your Higher Self to show you how your body feels when something is good for you, or right for you. You may get physical sensations, pictures, sounds, words, or just a hunch. Then ask how it feels when something isn't right for you. What does your body feel like, is there a smell or taste to it, or perhaps a sound or image comes to you. You can move back and forth between these states to get a stronger connection to your own signals. Doing this exercise every so often strengthens your connection to your Higher Self and your trust in your intuition deepens. A good exercise to do when you're caught up in shoulds. It's time to quit shoulding on yourself.

To find your natural rhythm is not that easy if you have a very scheduled life. It almost requires a freedom to flow with the day. But you can always start practicing on days off or during unscheduled time. Mostly it's about tuning into what you feel like doing or being in the moment. Some people do well with repetitive structure, where there is an order to each day. Others work in bursts with deep rest periods between the bursts. We have different needs for time with people and time alone. My equation doesn't look like your equation. For optimal functioning it's important to honor our natural pace. Ignore it too long and unwellness results. When I worked in the corporate world, I was always tired in the morning, and didn't feel like I was really there before 10 o'clock. Until I moved to France, that is. I lived close to work and we started later. I could sleep until 7 am, and for the first time I wasn't tired going to work! Imagine how many people are out there going against their natural cycle! For others it may be the opposite, they thrive on being up with the rooster!

To work with our natural gifts and talents is important for our well being. Being forced into jobs or structures that aren't congruent with who we are at a deeper level can be debilitating. We need to be able to use our natural talent at least 75% of the time. Sure, all lives have less favorite tasks that are a necessity for doing earth plane, just don't let them take over. So how do you know what your natural gifts are? Good question. Here are some detective games to play.

Play Detective

When you were young, what did you do? What did you play or pretend to be? Take a few moments and remember happy, contented times. What were you doing? Keep asking and be with the memories, keep looking until you find several. Most of you will notice there are certain skills or tendencies contained in your childhood memories. You don't have to restrict yourself to childhood. Notice what recurs. What skills are you using, what is it that fascinates you? I think it's important to work with something we are curious about, something that excites us. Ask your Higher Self to show you what is good for your life energy. The Hawaiian Hunas aim to follow the path that has most life energy. Working with your natural gifts in a way that is congruent with you will put you on the path of highest life energy.

Highest life energy doesn't mean running around like a banny rooster, rather it's an internal state of being, sort of quietly electrified.

Money Matters

I've met few therapists and workshop leaders who knew how to calculate what to charge so they can make a living doing what they love to do. So here's my version. If your inclination is to skip this chapter because you find it difficult to deal with money and mathematics, stop. Let yourself be with your resistance and work this chapter over and over until you get it. Use therapy to work through the issues that come up. Form a self help group and use the exercises in this book to break through into abundance.

Let's start with the therapist who works with individual clients. If you worked 40 hours per week and the year has 52 weeks, then there are 2080 hours per year. Can you work 52 weeks per year? Of course not. Holidays take away about two weeks, vacation takes away five weeks, continuing education takes away two weeks, perhaps you get sick and there go another few weeks. Here in Sweden we figure we have about 9 months out of 12 to make a living. A month is lost at Christmas and the other two months are summer and other holidays. So of the 2080 hours we started with, there are really only 3/4 or 75% of that available = 1560 available hours for a year.

Next issue is billable hours. Can you bill clients for all 1560 hours? No, the time you spent between clients, answering the phone, doing bookkeeping and taxes, doing marketing and explaining what you do and how you work are not billable to anyone. So all those hours need to be baked into your price. A general rule for consultants is that 50% of available time is billable to clients. There is also a limit to how many sessions and clients you can do in a week and stay fresh, we can work intensely for short periods, but you need to base your pricing on what is a sustainable pace year after year. The massage therapists I've known who've been in the business for 15 - 20 years consistently say that 3 max 4 clients per day is a sustainable pace.

Ok, so of the 1560 available hours we can only bill half or 50% = 780 billable hours per year.

Next, we'll need to calculate the net income after taxes and business expenses. I'm going to do an example using the Swedish tax rates, we have the highest taxes in the world, so it can only get better for the rest you. Just substitute your country and state tax rates as well as your local currency. At the time of this writing Sweden's currency is SEK or crowns, and the value of a crown is equal to 9 - 10 euro (€) or dollar (US$) and about 15£ (UK).

If I charge a rate of 700 SEK/hour (note this is for a 60 minute session, for a 45 minute session it would be 525 SEK) and multiply by 780 billable hours per year = 546.000 SEK per year. This is my gross income.

From the gross income of 546.000 SEK I need to subtract sales tax, or VAT as it is called in Europe. In Sweden it is 25% or 1/4 = 136.500. So I subtract 136.500 from 546.000 leaving me with 409.500 SEK.

Next I deduct my business expenses, such as office rent, supplies, telephone, computer equipment, advertising, marketing, continuing education, tax and legal advice etc. The last few years my business expenses have averaged 40.000 SEK per year. When I subtract that from 409.500 I am left with 369.500 SEK.

It's now time to deduct self employment tax or social taxes. In Sweden it's almost 33%, so for ease of calculation I'll use 33% which is about 1/3. So 33% of 369.500 = 121.935.

In Sweden the income tax is 30% up to a salary of about 25.000 per month or 300.000 per year. Then it goes up to 50%. For ease of calculation lets use 30% of 369.500 = 110.850.

Subtracting 121.935 and 110.850 from 369.500 leaves 136.715. This is your net spendable income, which spread out over 12 months is equal to 11.390 SEK per month for your personal expenses.

The actual calculation is a bit more complicated, but you get the general idea. To get a more exact calculation I used the internet calculation program provided by the Swedish Tax authorities at www.rsv.se and plotted the results:

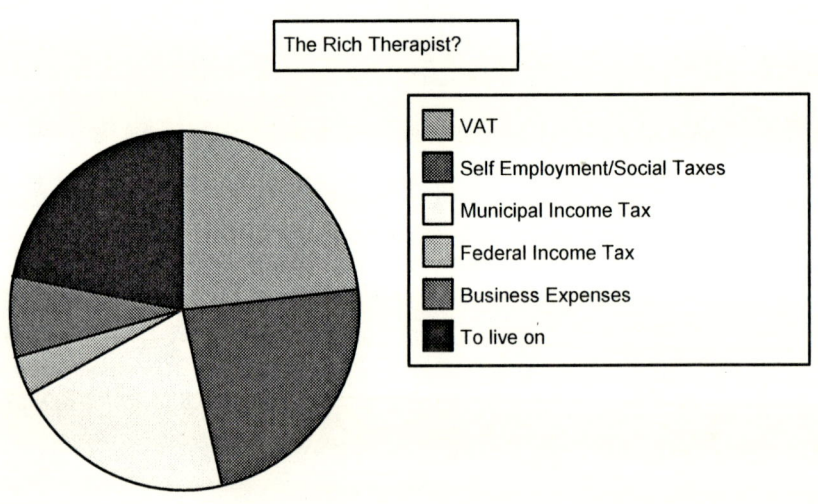

The Rich Therapist?

- VAT
- Self Employment/Social Taxes
- Municipal Income Tax
- Federal Income Tax
- Business Expenses
- To live on

About 70% of the income goes to taxes in the example above for Sweden. As a comparison, my colleagues in the State of Washington, USA pay about 50% of their income in taxes.

There, the B & O or Business and Occupation Tax is applied on gross income.

If you thought you'd get rich as a therapist, think again. So how can so many in this business charge so little? The answer I found, is that if you look closer, this is not their only source of income, in other words, they are not making a living at it. Is this what you want?

For workshop leaders the calculation is similar, but the expenses are generally greater and you spend even more time responding to inquiries and doing marketing. Don't forget to take into account the prep time, workshop space rental and all the extra organizing and arranging. For some reason it's easier to charge more for weekend and longer workshops than it is for weekly groups or evening courses.

Marketing

Mention sales and marketing and most therapists run for the door. This is not why we chose this profession. But, you can't get away from it. To run a business, you have to somehow make yourself known to the marketplace.

I am not an expert on this subject, nor particularly good at it. I would rather do, than talk about what I do. I've worked hard at finding ways to present what I do in an understandable fashion that is congruent with who I am. I keep trying different ways to connect with potential clients. There are many ways to go about selling yourself. You won't have the energy to do them all at the same time. I suggest you take one method and do that for a while, then recharge and try another method. Some tasks will be easier than others, others will bear more fruit. Look at it as a growth opportunity and get some therapy if it gets too difficult.

Decide on a business name. I was given the name Divine Design by my Higher Self and hesitated initially as it felt too pretentious, but it persisted. Now it feels really right.

Clients need to be able to get a hold of you and leave a message when you are busy with other clients. Get voice messaging or an answering machine. Have a phone number that is only for you and your business. Make the message personal and informative without getting too cute or weird.

Print up some business cards. The ones you create on the computer work just fine.

Do you need a website? Not necessarily, but I find it very helpful. Most people that now call have already looked on the website and read about me and what I do. So their questions are different, they are further along on the buying path. Before I had a website, people would call cold and I could easily spend an hour on the phone just covering the basics, and then I would send them a brochure and articles, which meant there would be yet another follow up, just to get to where we now start.

If you are reasonably computer literate, it's not that hard to make your own site. There are programs like Adobe Go Live that make the task easier. You can hire the work done, but it can quickly get expensive, especially if you make a lot of changes and updates. I'm trying to put basic information on my site and then send out emails to a subscriber list with course dates or other special information.

Printing brochures used to be an expensive proposition. Now you can easily make your own on your home computer. I use regular copy paper in some shade that prints well and is kind to the eyes when you to read it. I recommend you write it in your own words, because then it rings true to who you are. A friend of mine commented on my last brochure that it really resonated, she could really feel that I spoke from experience. She had read similar words in many other brochures about emotions and the physical body, but it was as if they were coming from a mental or more academic place than what I had written. Putting your picture on the brochure helps the client get a feel for who you are.

I think that the client buys you as a person and that the techniques you use are secondary to their decision. They are more interested in what you can help them with, who you are and what you have been through. That you are well trained and a professional is another decision criteria for most clients.

Giving talks in front of groups is another way to present yourself and your services. I've discovered I do best when I am present and just speak in the flow and let God fill me with words. It's taken some practice to get there, but once I've checked in with the group and got a feel for where they are at, it's surprisingly easy. I'm really lousy at prepared speeches using notecards and overheads. I used to struggle and fret and it invariably came off lifeless and flat. But we are all different, experiment until you find what works for you. Taking presentation seminars and classes give you valuable ideas to try. Everyone gets nervous at the beginning. You can't sleep the night before, your legs shake, your teeth rattle, your heart is pounding, you feel like vomiting and you wonder how you are going to keep your voice steady - don't worry, it will pass, once you get started it calms down, and it gets easier the more you practice.

Doing evening classes or study circles is another way to get known and a great way to practice your skills. You won't get rich doing it. For some reason people won't pay very much for an evening class. The same material presented over a weekend could bring in several times the income.

I tried doing low introductory rates, but wouldn't recommend it. When I started charging regular rates, people complained that it was expensive. They didn't think of it as having gotten a substantial discount before, they reacted as if I had raised the rates. Start out where you need to be.

In the Money Matters chapter I only covered rates for privately paying clients. Next I'll discuss the corporate and government markets. How this works is a little different for each country as behavior and laws vary across the globe. I'll use Sweden as an example as it is my current arena to practice in.

Here the private market is very small. There are several reasons for this - high taxes, low salaries, socialized medicine and a reliance on the government to take care of you and make decisions for you. The invoicable sector as I refer to it consists of private companies, social security administration, government medical organization and municipalities. When you look at your markets, there are two main factors to consider - who has a need for your services and who controls the money.

Invoice clients can afford to and expect to pay a higher fee than private clients. Here private rates are quoted inclusive of VAT and invoice rates exclusive of VAT. This is because all businesses can deduct outgoing VAT from their incoming sales VAT. My rates for a 45 minute session is 525 SEK for private clients and 900 SEK for invoice clients, which makes for a factor of 0,58 (=525/900).

Private companies that care about their employees may offer health benefits like gym membership or massage. Some pay for therapy, especially if the person in need is a high paid executive. Some companies bring in motivational speakers for conferences to speak on health and lifestyle topics. The government sector also employs a vast number of people who could use our help in one way or another.

The social security administration is responsible for paying out sick leave and rehabilitation from long term leave. Each region goes out for bids about every other year. Lots of paperwork but worth the effort if you can get a contract.

The unemployment administration sends lots of unemployed through training programs and schools. They also are responsible for retraining those on long term leave. They too go out for bids approximately every other year, but also buy up individual training programs locally.

The government medical organization is responsible for medical and psychiatric care. Only licensed professionals that fall under the regulation of the government are included in their services. What is needed is a dialogue between the regulated and non-regulated sectors.

The municipalities are responsible for welfare and addiction rehabilitation. They too rely on government licensed professionals.

Trying to get into the system in Sweden is a bit like Catch 22. For a method to be approved so you can be licensed in it, the training first has to exist as a college or university program. Then the legislature has to change the law to include this method within the official regulated system.

Selling your services to the invoice sector is a longer process, but a more profitable one in the long run.

Finding your niche may take awhile and it may also change over time. Most marketing experts recommend you clearly define a target market and focus like a laser on selling to that market.

Advertising costs a lot of money and the results are questionable. To be effective you need to run the ad repetitively over a long period of time, so that the message gets through. When they need your services, which may be several years down the road, you want them to automatically think of you. Being in the yellow pages may help establish you. Around here people use the little local phone books, so that is where one needs to advertise.

When a prospective client calls, ask them how they heard about you. It will help you understand what has worked. What has happened for me is that they have heard of me in several different ways, perhaps gone to one of my talks, then read an article about me in the paper and then saw me listed in the yellow pages. Point is they didn't call the first time they heard of me, but after the third or fourth.

Doing mailings keeps you visible, but is expensive. I now do an email list and occasionally call or mail those not on the internet.

Getting written about in newspapers and magazine is great publicity. It also establishes your credibility. Ask if you may publish the text of the article on your website. What someone else says about you packs a bigger punch than anything you say yourself. This is why it is so hard to sell therapy services. Satisfied clients and word of mouth is absolutely the best advertising you can get. Some practitioners publish testimonials on their websites and in their brochures.

Participating in fairs is another way to gain visibility. I stay away from the new age fairs as they tend to be too airy fairy. But locally we had an open house where therapists and teachers each had a booth with information materials and we also gave 30 minute presentations of our work in an adjoining conference room. It was a very successful format and well received.

I run my business out of my home so I have a sign on my house with business name, phone number and website address. The country road that passes by my house is well travelled, so I also have a store sidewalk display sign where I can change the message. It gets seen and read. On the back of my car I have a decal with my website address.

Depending on what you do, making up T-shirts connected to your business may work. Either for you to wear or to sell/hand out to clients. When I wear a T-shirt from a therapy conference I often get asked - what is that? Some of us don't mind being a walking advertisement.

If you are really ambitious, have a lot to say, or have a Higher Self that nudges you, writing a book is a great marketing tool. Sure it takes a long time to write and brings up even more issues for you to work through, but it establishes your credibility in a whole different way. It helps people understand your philosophy. It helps prospective clients and students decide if your program is what they want.

Being active in the local community and participating in networks is another way to get known. The networks I've found most productive are those where our businesses complement each other.

Training Program

How is a good training program arranged? I have a few ideas.

We all come into the program with different levels of experience, education and different goals. Some may want to learn everything that I teach, others may want to deepen their knowledge in one small area. The amount of supervised practice we need also varies greatly. This is why I believe in creating individual training programs that are designed around the individuals goals and prior level of experience, and that the training can be adjusted as progress is made.

Important components of a training program are:

Professional Workshops with a combination of theory and practice. Repeating workshops is an excellent way to anchor understanding of material, we rarely take in all that is presented the first time through. Workshops are also excellent places to make friends and for building networks. Workshop length can vary from a couple of days over a weekend to longer intensives. If participants have far to travel, doing a few longer intensives in a year may be better than weekend get togethers once a month. Each workshop needs to be long enough to move through substantial material. There needs to be sufficient amount of time between workshops for practice, yet the next workshop needs to come soon enough to keep the interest alive. With each subsequent workshop material is anchored and reviewed, and new material is introduced at a digestible pace.

Supervised Practice of all work while in training. Having a mentor who reviews all your work is essential to your success. Your mentor supports you by giving feedback, helping you think through what you may do different next time, gives you pats on the back for doing the right thing or making appropriate observations. Your mentor is there to guide your progress. Some disciplines have a tradition of lifelong mentor relationships. Just because you get a certificate on the wall doesn't mean you are "finished". We never finish learning and growing. Somewhere between 200 to 300 supervised individual sessions is needed to get a thorough grasp of the material. For those wanting to work with groups, have the trainee start weekly groups when they have made enough progress and supervise for at least six months. Or have the trainee pick about twelve clients that they work with individually and in group for about a year.

Own Development is absolutely key in becoming a good therapist or group facilitator. Getting regular trades, weekly or twice a month is recommended. To be able to work effectively with others, you need to break through your own issues. How can you expect to take a client where you haven't been able to go? Learning to surrender and letting the process swallow you up may be the most important tool you can acquire. When I trade with my colleagues from other countries we get together for a week or two, sometimes we do a combination therapy/vacation trip. If we are just doing therapy, one of us gets to be client before lunch, then we switch for the afternoon sessions. We've found it works better than flip-flopping every hour.

Expanding Experience to include taking therapy from other disciplines and attending other workshops. Understanding how our colleagues work is important, and is helpful when you need to refer a client to someone else. Most of us end up with a synthesis of several teachers and disciplines approaches, we harvest from several sources.

Assisting at Workshops helps develop your group skills, deepens your understanding of the material and builds relationships with other practitioners. Watching more experienced mentors work with clients at a workshop is a tremendous learning opportunity.

Business Training is rarely included in the professional training of therapists, but the hard truth is that we do not become employees. If we want to work with therapy and personal growth, we have to run our own businesses. You do not need to be an expert in business matters, but you need to know enough about bookkeeping, taxes, marketing and legal matters to be effective. Even if you hire someone to do your books, it's important to have some basic understanding. In countries where the private market is small, you'll need to learn how to market your services to the corporate and government sector.

Continuing Education and Development is needed to help you keep growing as a human being, and it's important to stay current with developments in the field. Sharing research and discoveries with others in your profession is an exciting part of the journey. Personally I'd prefer to have network get togethers to share experiences, dialogue about issues and try some new approaches.

To do a training program for the material presented in this book may take 3 - 5 years. For more information about current programs and other news check out my website at www.divinedesign.nu.

Choosing a Therapist

Just like life is a treasure hunt, so goes the search for a good therapist. When you are a mess it's not easy to be clear if someone is good for you, and you are bound to make some mistakes. Sometimes you'll choose a therapist that is a mirror of an unhealthy relationship and your task will be to say no thanks - done that, been there, got the t-shirt - and head out the door as fast as you can.

So how can you tell? The answer is you can't know for sure until you try them out. Look at their picture. Does this look like the kind of person you would like to become? Would you feel safe entrusting them with your deepest secrets? When you talk to them, do you feel respected and honored? If they try to push you, or make you feel dependent, act authoritative and only they know what's best for you, then I would steer clear. If they keep backing off and say you are not ready, we'll take that next time, go find another therapist.

You need someone who will work with you for your highest good. Someone who is not afraid to go where you need to go.

Occasionally make an evaluation. What is the effect of the therapy? Has my life changed? Have I changed? Are my behavior patterns changed or am I still stuck in the same patterns? The effect of therapy is not necessarily linked to dramatic sessions. Some of the biggest real changes come after very subtle and soft work. Beware of becoming a drama addict. As we heal, there is less and less drama in our lives and that is our natural state, to be in the natural flow of life.

Is your therapist real? Can he/she fall apart and be human? Look out for the gurus who claim to have cleared all their stuff - I've run into a few with really deep unresolved traumas, and they can be tricky to detach from without getting slimed with guilt.

Does your therapist have a social life and friends, in other words is this person relatively normal? You need a therapist who is a flesh and blood human being, someone who is real. Ask yourself, is this person good for me? Do they really know what they are talking about? Does it come from experience or is it just theory? Do they know what they are doing?

What is their motivation for helping me? When I work I tune into my Higher Self and ask that whatever happens be for the highest good of the client or group I am working with. This helps keep the ego out of the way and opens the way for the unexpected to happen. When intuition is allowed to flow freely, magic can occur.

I personally don't care to be sold a bunch of products in addition to therapy. A few select items is one thing, but often the cost of the products is more than the session. And the focus tends to gets shifted away from the real reason you are there.

The same criteria is also useful for finding a teacher.

Further Meditations

The importance of a daily plug-in to Source can not be overemphasized. Twenty minutes is all that is required - daily. Will change happen overnight? No, it is generally agreed that it takes 1000 days or about three years of daily meditation to achieve a shift in consciousness. My own experience bears this out. Although I felt a benefit from the very start of my meditation practice, there was a definite difference after three years. My thinking was different. I felt whole.

Meditation does not need to be complicated. To start, you may need to practice progressive relaxation, but eventually your being becomes so conditioned that the meditative state comes naturally and easily when you sit or lie down.

Higher Self Meditation
The most basic of meditations is to simply be with your Higher Self. Just state I now connect to my Higher Self and keep your attention focused inward. Keep breathing gently and relax. Focus on being, not doing, that's the whole point.

Valley of Peace Meditation

For further exploration take yourself to the Valley of Peace, located in the sacral chakra. This is where I become aware of the presence of Jesus, you may experience something else that represents peace to you.

Garden of Quan Yin Meditation

Quan Yin is the eastern goddess of mercy and compassion. I experience her garden in my heart chakra. Contemplate the qualities mercy, compassion and love as you stroll through the garden. Sit by a quiet stream and bask in the presence of Quan Yin.

Concept Meditation

In writing this book I discovered I had some unresolved issues about success. I used concept meditation to help move through my blocks. I meditated on the concept of success. You can meditate on any concept, for example power, worth, charity etc. In the meditative state, focus your awareness on the concept and notice how your body responds, your breath, your thoughts. Be with the process until it feels complete. At first, great sadness came to me. After the tears, quiet. The next session, incredible fear in my solar plexus, and it was hard to breathe. I remembered times of great fear and confusion when money had come into my life and how panicky I felt. The fear was pounding alternately on the left and right hand sides of my solar plexus, then that shifted. The next session I felt my sacral chakra, questions of worth surfaced. As I allowed myself to be with each feeling, it shifted and dissolved, until it felt good to have success and money come into my life.

The concept meditation works like an affirmation. When you affirm something positive, the subconscious responds with all that doesn't match the affirmation, so we can clear that out. The same process happens when you contemplate a concept, you are affirming success or peace, and your subconscious brings to your attention all your beliefs and memories that aren't success or peace. It's just being helpful, and honestly - who wants to carry that muck around?

Success is so much more than money. It has a different meaning for each and every one of us. Why are we so frightened of being ourselves in all our glory? Perhaps because we have to grow and face the dragons to get there.

Few books of this sort ever talk about the sessions that weren't successful, or all the things you tried to get a client to break through that didn't work. It's easy to get the impression that every session is laden with emotional release and insight, or that every meditation is profound and enlightening. Truth is that there are many mundane sessions. Just like life, it's weekday most of the time. I believe that all those everyday type sessions, that weren't remarkable, are just as important as the spectacular ones. I suspect it is all those mundane sessions, plugging away at it, that eventually leads to the breakthrough. Too often, the person that tips the scale in that one session gets all the credit. I think it's important to acknowledge all the actions and helpers that made the breakthrough possible.

Letting go sounds so easy, yet it is probably the hardest thing to do. Most of us work very hard at it. After all it is scary. We got injured by letting go and letting someone else decide who we were. And only in letting go again can we heal. Therein lies the paradox.

About the Author

"Spiritual pioneer" said the astrologer when she looked at Eva Dillner's horoscope, with a focus on emotional release. Originally an engineer, Eva spent fifteen years in the corporate world working with project management and organizational change in the United States and France. Burned out by yet another downsizing, she left in 1991 and started training with the pioneers in the personal growth and therapy movement in the United States and Europe. She discovered the path back to life and calls her synthesis of emotional release therapy and spiritual growth "Life Therapy". In 1998 she started the company Divine Design in Sweden and has been featured in major articles in the local as well as national press - read more on www.divinedesign.nu.

Printed in the United Kingdom
by Lightning Source UK Ltd.
9585700001B